HOOTERS

BY TED TALLY

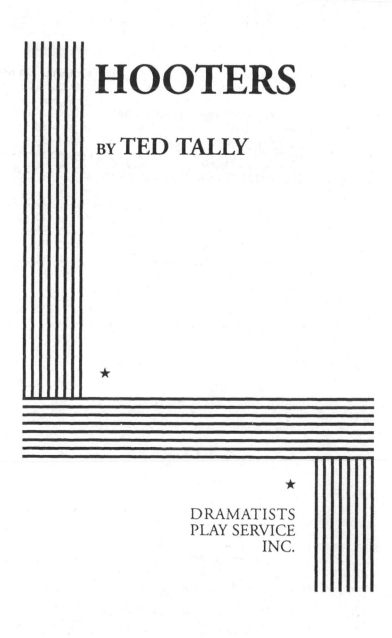

DRAMATISTS
PLAY SERVICE
INC.

For Gary & Mary

HOOTERS was first performed April 18th, 1978 at Playwright's Horizons in New York City. It was directed by Gary Pearle. The setting was designed by Charles McCarry, the costumes by Elizabeth Palmer, and the lighting by Frances Aronson. Susanna Styron was assistant to the director; Lisa Baker was production stage manager.

The cast was as follows:

CLINT	Michael Kaufman
RICKY	Victor Bevine
RONDA	Erika Petersen
CHERYL	Christine Lahti

AUTHOR'S NOTE: In the original production of the play, a tape of soft-rock songs was used as pre-show music, as well as during intermission and curtain calls. Act One blackouts were covered either by songs or by a tape of drum riffs, and Act Two blackouts were covered by a tape of ocean surf.

CHARACTERS

CLINT

RICKY

RONDA

CHERYL

The men are both 19. Ronda is 22, and Cheryl is 25.

SETTING

A motel on Cape Cod, and the beach nearby.

A late-summer weekend. The present.

Center stage, a raised platform made of weathered gray planking. On this is constructed an entire motel room interior, which will double as both the men's room and the women's.

There are no walls. Access to the room is by boardwalk-style ramps. The outside door is understood to be Offstage Right, and the bathroom Offstage Left. The furnishings—two twin beds, a dresser with a mirror, two standing lamps, a wastebasket, and a TV—are typical of an ordinary motel room, which is to say innocuous in design and garish in color. However they feel somewhat out of place, imposed on what we suspect to be an older motel.

Completely surrounding this platform, and extending well Downstage to create a separate playing space, are sand dunes, flat sandy patches, and tall beach grass. Access to the beach is by steps far Right which lead up to a boardwalk. This boardwalk runs along the Upstage edge, above the motel room, and goes off Up Left.

A cyclorama is thrown around the rear perimeter of the stage, further enhancing our sense of open space and sky. (In the New York production, a photo-mural of a beach scene, mounted on an old fashioned billboard, was substituted for a cyclorama. See photo.)

HOOTERS

ACT ONE

Scene One. Friday Evening.

The men's motel room.

Clint enters, struggling with the weight of a large styrofoam cooler. He drops it with a gasp on one of the beds. He sits, opens the cooler, takes out a beer. He opens it and drinks.

RICKY. (*Offstage.*) Did you see that?
CLINT. See what?
RICKY. (*Off.*) Incredible!
CLINT. See what?
RICKY. (*Off.*) Parking lot! Jesus!
CLINT. See *what*? (*Ricky enters, carrying two suitcases, an airline bag, and a suit bag.*)
RICKY. Right after we pulled in!
CLINT. Where?
RICKY. The window!
CLINT. Where?
RICKY. Hurry up! (*Ricky is dropping bags in a wild flurry as he races for the "window," D. C. Clint tries to catch a falling suitcase and misses it.*)
CLINT. Hey, watch it!
RICKY. (*Looking out.*) Where are you, I know you're out there, come on . . .
CLINT. My binoculars are in here!
RICKY. (*Points.*) There, right there! Peace on earth, good will to men. (*The next two lines overlap.*)
CLINT. Just throw my goddam binoculars down next time like they were made out of rubber why don't you?
RICKY. Will you shut up already and just come over here and take a look at this?

7

CLINT. Jerkwad.

RICKY. And bring the binoculars! (*Clint fumbles in his suitcase, pulls out binoculars, hurries to the "window."*)

CLINT. What's the big deal?

RICKY. That! Will you look at that? Un-be-lievable.

CLINT. Where?

RICKY. Behind the green *Camaro!* What are you, blind? Hurry up, it's on the hoof!

CLINT. Where's the *Camaro,* for Christ's sake?

RICKY. Big tree—left side—over a little—

CLINT. I see it! I see the green *Camaro!* (*Pause.*) I don't see anything else.

RICKY. (*Stares out, relaxes.*) Skip it.

CLINT. That's it? A green *Camaro?*

RICKY. Skip it, it's gone. You'll never see it again for the rest of your life.

CLINT. I never saw it the first time! (*Ricky crosses, sprawls out on a bed.*)

RICKY. You had your chance and you blew it.

CLINT. (*Still peering through binoculars.*) Where? (*Pause.*) You mean that fat number in the sweatshirt?

RICKY. *Wrong.*

CLINT. You broke my Swiss binoculars just to show me some fat broad in a Snoopy sweatshirt?

RICKY. Idiot! I'm talking masterpiece and all you can see is the livestock. Throw me a beer.

CLINT. Well, I don't see anything.

RICKY. Throw me a beer.

CLINT. Throw yourself a beer!

RICKY. C'mon sport. (*Clint opens cooler, gets a beer and tosses it to Ricky. Then he sits on the other bed and examines his binoculars.*)

CLINT. If you'll pardon me saying so, I think you're full of it. And I don't even believe there *was* anything.

RICKY. (*Pause.*) Well?

CLINT. I think they're okay.

RICKY. Will you forget the stupid binoculars?

CLINT. These things are *Zeiss,* buddy, in case you never heard of that.

RICKY. No, I never heard of that.

8

CLINT. Well maybe if you were still in school you'd hear about a few things for a change.

RICKY. Oh yeah? Sure. What are you, *majoring* in binoculars? Look, you want to hear about this or not, cause you know you do, only you just can't stand to be too *interested*, cause that's not cool for college types or something.

CLINT. I really don't give a flying fart.

RICKY. Course not.

CLINT. (*Pause.*) It's not as if I even did, cause I don't.

RICKY. Sure. (*Pause.*) Five foot ten.

CLINT. Get out.

RICKY. I swear to God. Twenty-five or twenty-six years old.

CLINT. (*Whistles.*) Jesus. I never made it with an older womàn. Have you?

RICKY. Plenty of times.

CLINT. And?

RICKY. And, maybe you weren't aware, but there's a very interesting statistic that women that age and up are just beginning to hit their sexual potential.

CLINT. I know how they feel.

RICKY. Ha! For you it was fourteen. You're five years over the hill already.

CLINT. What color hair did she have?

RICKY. Well—brown.

CLINT. Boring, in other words.

RICKY. Hair okay, but nothing to write home about.

CLINT. What color eyes?

RICKY. I don't know—big! What's all this color business?

CLINT. Physique?

RICKY. Now you're talking. *Great* physique—A minus on the lungs.

CLINT. Good knockers, huh?

RICKY. Very good hooters.

CLINT. *Hooters!?*

RICKY. Honk honk!

CLINT. Jesus, I haven't heard that word since high school.

RICKY. Well it's only been a year. You make it sound like World War II or something. (*They have begun unpacking their suitcases.*)

CLINT. What about her legs?

RICKY. Endless.

CLINT. What about her ass?

RICKY. Clint, try not to be so crude. You're talking about the woman I love.

CLINT. In other words, she's got a *great* ass.

RICKY. Hey hey hey!

CLINT. Whattya say?

RICKY. Okay, hold it a minute: Her face. Clint, I can't even find the words. Never before seen in our galaxy.

CLINT. Yeah?

RICKY. *Overall* rating—including the face—are you ready?

CLINT. Overall.

RICKY. (*Takes a breath.*) A Ten.

CLINT. (*Pause.*) Are you out of your mind?

RICKY. A definite Ten.

CLINT. Are you crazy?

RICKY. From the Russian judge, a nine-point eight, but I gotta say an All-American Ten.

CLINT. With boring hair and A minus hooters?

RICKY. I'm talking overall effect. The sum is more than the parts.

CLINT. Ricky, there is no such thing. Tens are only in your mind.

RICKY. Nadia Comaneci was a Ten. This is a Ten.

CLINT. You're just saying that because I didn't see her.

RICKY. One-Oh.

CLINT. You're making it up.

RICKY. I stand by my judgement.

CLINT. You must mean a Nine. Surely you mean a high Nine, which in itself is unbelievable.

RICKY. I think we ought to recognize perfection when it floats by us.

CLINT. You're delirious!

RICKY. Ah, *now* he wakes up. Don't get too many Tens around the dorm, huh? But I saw one here. You're just pissed you didn't.

CLINT. Nobody's *ever* seen a Ten! (*Pause.*) The whole idea of Tenhood loses its meaning if anybody ever sees one!

RICKY. I not only saw her.

CLINT. What do you mean?

RICKY. I more than just saw her.

CLINT. What?

RICKY. I nodded to her.

CLINT. You did *what?*

RICKY. You heard me, ace.

CLINT. (*Pause.*) Did you—talk to her?

RICKY. What do you think, I wanted to scare her off? Jesus!

CLINT. Okay!

RICKY. We looked. I nodded. (*Pause.*) Then I gave her the eye.

CLINT. Get out of here!

RICKY. No, man.

CLINT. You gave her the eye?

RICKY. Well, I sort of squinted. The sun was in my eyes. I was carrying all our junk.

CLINT. You didn't do that thing with your tongue, did you?

RICKY. No!

CLINT. If you did that tongue thing I'll murder you.

RICKY. I didn't!

CLINT. Because you may think that's cool, but it makes you look like a rattlesnake.

RICKY. Will you grow up? I just gave her the eye.

CLINT. What did she do?

RICKY. She sort of smiled.

CLINT. Are you kidding? She was *nice*?

RICKY. It's true. I swear to God she's got the hots for me.

CLINT. Oh man, now I know you're full of it! (*Pause.*) Did she *say* anything? What did she say?

RICKY. She was playing it a little cool, but a guy can tell.

CLINT. Well what did she say?

RICKY. This and that.

CLINT. No, man, *c'mon!*

RICKY. Just stuff. Excuse me, could you move your car you're blocking me in and stuff. But *nice.*

CLINT. Oh God, I can *hear* her! She's got this voice like hot maple syrup in February . . .

RICKY. Yeah. So then I moved the car and—

CLINT. She opens her mouth, her beautiful gorgeous twenty-five year old mouth, and out comes this—*sound*—

RICKY. Whatever. So then—

CLINT. Like a cool breeze when you've worked up a sweat—like a—

RICKY. Who's telling this?

CLINT. Promise me she's not a c.t.

RICKY. No way, Renee. This girl puts out, I can tell.

11

CLINT. Cause if she's a Ten and a c.t., I'm going to go in*sane*. There won't be any reason to go on living.

RICKY. I'm telling you, she puts *out*.

CLINT. Are you crazy? A Ten that puts out?

RICKY. The mind boggles, doesn't it?

CLINT. (*Grabbing binoculars, hurrying back to window.*) A Ten that puts out—and is staying right here in this motel?

RICKY. Hey man, it's the Cod, right? What'd I tell you? We're here five minutes and a Ten is trolling her ass through the goddam parking lot.

CLINT. The Cape, Ricky. Not "the Cod." And a real Ten wouldn't troll her ass through any parking lot. She'd be too nice.

RICKY. Well maybe there's two kinds of Tens, Mr. Coolness, did you ever stop to think about that? Maybe there's the nice girl kind, sort of the skinny wispy model, and then maybe there's another kind that will chew through you like a Black and Decker chainsaw. And maybe—I say just maybe—what we've got here is the kind with teeth.

CLINT. A minus on the hooters, right?

RICKY. Like she got hit in the back by a pair of bazooka shells.

CLINT. Jesus.

RICKY. Jesus H.

CLINT. This is it, huh? A Ten. Oh wow . . .

RICKY. Hey—hey Clint—just like old times, huh?

CLINT. You said it, pal.

RICKY. All *right!* Only this time with a Ten!

CLINT. And how many of *those* were there at Dwight D. Eisenhower Senior High?

RICKY and CLINT. (*Together.*) Zilch!

RICKY. A Ten!

CLINT. A Ten!

RICKY. An Ab-so-lute Ten . . .

(Blackout.)

Scene Two. Friday Evening.

The women's motel room. Cheryl is unpacking her suitcase. Ronda is at the window.

RONDA. I think they're in that last room on the other wing. There's a light on.

CHERYL. You see them?

RONDA. No. Wait a minute—now I do. One of them's just come to the window. (*Pause.*) Oh no—you're not going to believe this . . .

CHERYL. What.

RONDA. One of them is standing at the window with a pair of binoculars.

CHERYL. You're kidding.

RONDA. I kid you not.

CHERYL. Which one is it—the cute one or the other one?

RONDA. I didn't know there was a cute one.

CHERYL. The one I made move their car.

RONDA. He seemed very shallow to me.

CHERYL. How can you tell that from a ten-second glimpse in a parking lot?

RONDA. He had a shallow walk.

CHERYL. I don't know. He had a cute ass. (*She crosses, looks out.*)

RONDA. Cheryl, his ass is beside the point. That little twirp deliberately parked that car to block us in. Don't let him see you!

CHERYL. Okay, okay! Why would he do that?

RONDA. To have an excuse to talk to us, dummy.

CHERYL. But he didn't.

RONDA. Too nervous. He took one look at you and swallowed his gum.

CHERYL. They're just kids.

RONDA. Could you believe the way he stood there staring? The *nerve* on that guy. He's looking this way—duck! (*Ronda dives down to the floor. Cheryl remains standing.*)

CHERYL. Oh for Pete's sake.

RONDA. Get down, he'll see you!

CHERYL. This is definitely the cute one—the other one had different hair.

RONDA. (*Pause.*) I wish you'd get down here. I feel ridiculous.

CHERYL. You look ridiculous.

RONDA. Well, if you're just going to stand there, making a perfect target, then I'm going to stand up too.

CHERYL. It's okay, I think they're turning in.

RONDA. (*Rising.*) Thank goodness. I've got grime all over my knees. (*Cheryl goes back to her unpacking.*)
CHERYL. Better not stand in front of the light. He may come back with a telescope.
RONDA. Let him. I don't care.
CHERYL. Obviously!
RONDA. You know what these guys are like. Give 'em an inch and they want six.
CHERYL. I'll protect you, okay?
RONDA. (*Laughing.*) Get out of here. (*She takes a nightgown from her suitcase.*) You wouldn't believe how much dust is on this floor. I don't think this place has had a mop-and-glow since the Pilgrims. (*Ronda crosses into bathroom to change for bed.*)
CHERYL. Welcome to the Pequod Inn.
RONDA. (*Off.*) I thought you said this place was quaint.
CHERYL. It is.
RONDA. (*Off.*) Well, it's falling apart. I guess it's the same thing.
CHERYL. You don't like it? (*Cheryl takes her diaphragm, in its case, out of her overnight bag and looks for a place to hide it. She finally settles on wrapping it in some underwear and putting it in a drawer of the dresser.*)
RONDA. (*Off.*) You must've been here with some guy.
CHERYL. David, as a matter of fact.
RONDA. (*Off.*) Figures. He *would* be into this total New England lobster-trap motif.
CHERYL. He was really mad when he saw there was a TV in our room. Believe it?
RONDA. (*Off.*) Go figure.
CHERYL. If it's not from the 18th century it's too newfangled. He'd like me better if I was 250 years old and had a steep price tag. (*Ronda re-enters from bathroom, wearing nightgown.*)
RONDA. He likes you too much as it is.
CHERYL. Did you know they're going to make him a vice president?
RONDA. Be still my heart.
CHERYL. He told me the other night over dinner.
RONDA. Was that the same night he popped the q?
CHERYL. Oh, God, practically in the same sentence. He laid out all his assets, one by one, and then proposed a merger. (*Ronda*

laughs.) I swear, sometimes it's like sleeping with a portfolio. And I know he means to be sweet, it's not that. He's just so goddam *organized.* (*Slight pause.*) He files his shirts in the closet.

RONDA. Go on.

CHERYL. I'm not kidding.

RONDA. By color or pattern?

CHERYL. Both. Now I ask you, do I really want to marry a guy who files his shirts?

RONDA. Sure. You could type his grocery lists.

CHERYL. I don't know, I don't know. He *is* nice. He's caring. And he's got an incredible wad of money.

RONDA. Those are all important traits.

CHERYL. I sound awful, don't I?

RONDA. But you do like him.

CHERYL. I like him a lot, I really do. I'm just not sure I ought to marry him, that's all. Could you hand me my cold cream? It's in that bag.

RONDA. (*Searching through makeup bag.*) Christ, Cher—look at all this junk you've got in here.

CHERYL. I couldn't spend another weekend with him, Ron. Not right now. He's too good at arguing his own case.

RONDA. You're like the Avon lady. Here.

CHERYL. Thanks.

RONDA. Moisturizer, clarifying lotion, tanning gel, pore minimizing fluid—what the hell is that?

CHERYL. That's very important. Makes the big pores look smaller, and the little pores look like they're not even there.

RONDA. (*Putting some on, experimentally.*) But then, if it blocks up your pores, how do they breathe?

CHERYL. They don't, I guess.

RONDA. Then doesn't all that gunk start to back up?

CHERYL. I guess.

RONDA. Then you break out again, right?

CHERYL. Oh, there's another one for that—right here. Made by the same company. "Opens the pores back up so you can see them again."

RONDA. Which brings us back to where we started.

CHERYL. (*Slight pause.*) You're right.

RONDA. It all seems so futile sometimes. (*Pause.*) Is this a zit?

CHERYL. Where?

15

RONDA. Right here on my chin. Don't lie.

CHERYL. I think maybe.

RONDA. I knew it! It's those goddam Moby Dick fish sticks we had for dinner. By Monday I'll need a tube of caulk and a putty scraper.

CHERYL. Oh Ronnie.

RONDA. Where's that stuff that opens up the pores?

CHERYL. Hey, go easy. That's expensive.

RONDA. What do you care, you don't even need it. You've got perfect skin, you've got lashes and cheekbones. And hair! How come you even wear this garbage?

CHERYL. I don't know. I always have.

RONDA. There's no need for you to go through these bizarre rituals. You've already landed the Boy Wonder.

CHERYL. I don't just wear this stuff for him! I happen to like the way it makes me feel.

RONDA. Okay. (*She crosses, climbs into bed.*)

CHERYL. (*Slight pause.*) You know what I really resent about David?

RONDA. What?

CHERYL. There's this undertone, he's not even aware of it, that he's doing me this big *favor,* somehow. I mean he's this boy v.p. at the bank, and I'm just this *teller*—

RONDA. Not even a college graduate, God help us—

CHERYL. Just this poor little somebody he's got to rescue from a life of tellerdom.

RONDA. I wish somebody would rescue *me* from tellerdom. I hate the bank.

CHERYL. And he's really going to fix me up, you know? Give me some *focus.*

RONDA. Sure. Give you some kids is what he means.

CHERYL. But I really *like* him! I don't know what to do. He wants an answer, Ron.

RONDA. I know, it's on his schedule for Monday morning. "Eight o'clock—settle next fifty years." (*Pause.*) Hey, Cher, don't panic. We've got the whole weekend to think it over.

CHERYL. (*Smiles.*) Ron? Thanks.

RONDA. Oh, listen.

CHERYL. No, I just wanted to say.

RONDA. Don't have to.

16

CHERYL. For coming. You know—for putting up with me.

RONDA. Hey. Let's get up early and hit the beach.

CHERYL. Yeah. Sleep well, Ronnie. (*Cheryl turns off the lamp. Stage goes very dim. Cheryl runs through one or two quick exercises, preparing for bed. Pause. She looks at Ronda, then over at the window. She crosses quietly to the window.*)

RONDA. Where are you going?

CHERYL. I just thought I'd check up on cute-ass one last time.

RONDA. Oh Christ.

CHERYL. You know, see if he's tucked in snug.

RONDA. And?

CHERYL. You won't believe this.

RONDA. I believe it.

CHERYL. He's back.

RONDA. I'm not saying he's big on charm, but I give the kid high marks on persistence.

CHERYL. And cutes.

RONDA. If you say so.

CHERYL. Well. We need our sleep even if he doesn't need his.

RONDA. I'll say. (*Pause.*) Good thing *we're* not interested.

CHERYL. Good *night*, Ron.

(*Blackout.*)

Scene Three. Saturday Noon.

Sound of a transistor radio. Lights up on the beach.

Ricky is sitting, looking through binoculars. He wears swim trunks and sits on a towel. The cooler is beside him. He makes a slow sweep of the horizon with the binoculars.

Clint enters, also in swimwear and wearing sunglasses. He carries a cardboard box with food. He tries to speak to Ricky, but cannot be heard over the radio music. He crosses, turns off the radio.

CLINT. Well?

RICKY. I've got a maroon micro-bikini at two hundred yards . . .

17

one shoulder strap off on the bra . . . but I've had my eye on the second strap for at least ten minutes, and it doesn't look like it's gonna go.

CLINT. I got yours with mustard and ketchup. No pickle relish, and the fat sonofabitch ahead of me got the last of the onions.

RICKY. Christ, I don't see how in the world that thing stays up . . . by all the laws of gravity she oughtta be floppin' around in the surf, lookin' for her top half . . .

CLINT. Any sign of the Ten?

RICKY. No sign of the Ten. (*Pause.*) I do have a topless at fifty paces . . .

CLINT. (*Startled.*) Are you fu—

RICKY. But she couldn't be more than eight.

CLINT. Well—you know what they say.

RICKY. "Eight to eighty, blind, crippled or crazy."

CLINT. You hold out a lollipop and I'll grab her from behind.

RICKY. Hey hey hey.

CLINT. Whattya say.

RICKY. Actually . . . she's not that *bad.*

CLINT. This is ridiculous.

RICKY. Annhh. My nose is peeling.

CLINT. Put on some more goop.

RICKY. I hate laying in the sun. I get all sweaty. I get a rash.

CLINT. Maybe we oughtta go in the water. She didn't show by now, we oughtta go in the water.

RICKY. Take over for a minute while I take a food break. (*Ricky hands binoculars to Clint, reaches for a hotdog.*)

CLINT. (*Scanning through binoculars.*) Jesus, the kennels let out early today. (*Pause.*) I don't think she's gonna come out here this morning.

RICKY. She'll come out. We just have to be patient.

CLINT. She might be sitting in her room.

RICKY. Doing what?

CLINT. Watching the tube or something.

RICKY. Chicks don't come to the beach to watch tube. They come to the beach to get laid. She'll be here.

CLINT. She might've gone to some other beach.

RICKY. Well we can't stake out the whole coastline! This is the closest one to the motel. This hotdog sucks.

CLINT. Thanks. I'll walk all the way back and get you another one.

RICKY. Don't worry ace—we'll see her. It's not such a big place.

CLINT. I don't even believe she exists. I think she's like the white whale or something.

RICKY. The white whale existed.

CLINT. In a book! Big deal.

RICKY. It's the same thing, isn't it?

CLINT. Jerkwad.

RICKY. Put some of this stuff on my back. I feel like a goddam lobster.

CLINT: Put it on your own back! I'm not touching your back.

RICKY. Just a little bit along my shoulder blades where I can't reach. C'mon.

CLINT. Are you crazy? Somebody might be looking!

RICKY. (Pause.) So?

CLINT. So it's bad enough, two guys sitting together alone on a beach with no chicks, let alone if they're feeling each other up.

RICKY. I didn't say feel me up. I said put a little of this junk on my back.

CLINT. Man, you are so *naive!*

RICKY. What do you mean?

CLINT. How do you think we're ever gonna pick up any action if a chick sees something like that? You think the Ten is gonna give us the time of day with some guy's hands all over you? Christ— Fire Island!

RICKY. (Pause.) I never thought of that.

CLINT. Well you better think about it, because I have a feeling it may be cramping my style.

RICKY. You don't want to work as a team anymore? I thought we were in this together.

CLINT. We are in this together.

RICKY. Share and share alike.

CLINT. We are.

RICKY. What's mine is yours. Team spirit.

CLINT. We are a team.

RICKY. Because if you have that attitude we didn't even have to take a weekend together. I could've gone to Atlantic City—that's where the action is anyway.

19

CLINT. You're the one who wanted to go to the "Cod" in the first place! I wanted to go to Ocean Beach, so don't get huffy.

RICKY. I'm not huffy, I'm sunstroked.

CLINT. Well just ease up, for Christ's sake. (*Pause.*) I just think we might do a little better if you moved your towel over a little bit so people don't get the wrong impression. And when I say people I don't mean people. I mean *girls.*

RICKY. Just a little gap between us.

CLINT. Right.

RICKY. Sort of a buffer zone.

CLINT. Right.

RICKY. Well, okay, if you think that's better.

CLINT. I think that would look a lot better.

RICKY. Okay, how about over here? Is this far enough?

CLINT. A little further.

RICKY. How about here?

CLINT. That looks good.

RICKY. I'm glad you're satisfied.

CLINT. I am.

RICKY. Good. So am I.

CLINT. Good.

RICKY. I'll just stay right over here, and I'll do a little sunbathing.

CLINT. Good, you do that.

RICKY. I will. And I'll put my own goddam suntan lotion on.

CLINT. Fine. (*Silence.*)

RICKY. Are we allowed to talk, or is that too faggoty?

CLINT. You can talk as long as chicks aren't coming by. If I see some chicks coming along the beach, we'll have a signal.

RICKY. A signal?

CLINT. I'll cough once if they're dogs and it doesn't matter, and twice for something you should shut up because we might want to hit on it. Three coughs means they're out of range again.

RICKY. Cool! Four coughs could mean a chick who's kind of ugly but looks like she might have a nice personality, and five coughs means you got a piece of hotdog stuck in your throat.

CLINT. You got a better idea?

RICKY. What is this, some kind of college trip? The guys down at the frat cooked this up, or what?

CLINT. I don't see where your great plans are getting us any action, so what's wrong with just trying one of mine for a change?

RICKY. Some plan. Lying twelve feet apart and coughing. Sounds like a t.b. ward.

CLINT. Okay, just forget it.

RICKY. Maybe we'll get a couple of *nurses.*

CLINT. I don't know what you think you'd do with them if we did.

RICKY. Oh ho HO! I don't see where you're such a big stud all of a sudden, Mr. BMOC!

CLINT. Okay, just cool your tool, okay? You're getting brain fever or. something. Maybe you oughtta just go lie under an umbrella for awhile.

RICKY. I'm not even gonna talk to you anymore, cause I don't need this, you understand? I don't *need* this advice. Not from old "Clint the Splint," strikeout king of Eisenhower High. The only place you ever made time was in study hall! (*Pause. A slowly dawning realization.*) The *real* reason you want to break up the act is so you can have her all to yourself.

CLINT. That's ridiculous!

RICKY. I did spot her first, in case you're wondering.

CLINT. You're getting really paranoid.

RICKY. I'm keeping you in my sights at all time from now on.

CLINT. Just remember I have equal rights.

RICKY. If you're planning on sneaking out and asking her to go for a drink or something you can just forget it, because I'll be right on your heels.

CLINT. *I've* never even *seen* her!

RICKY. Right on your heels!

CLINT. She may not even be around anymore!

RICKY. I don't know how you could do that to your best buddy. I haven't even introduced you to this girl, and now you're practically planning to *marry* her. And don't tell me I'm paranoid, because you've changed, buster! You've *changed* from high school, and I know how your little brain is working. (*Cheryl and Ronda appear u. of the beach, on a boardwalk. They wear swimsuits and carry beachbags. They walk slowly down to the beach and across it, going behind Ricky, who doesn't see them. When Clint sees them, he coughs twice, but Ricky ignores the warning.*) Get rid of old Richard, right? Get her off alone and pour on this whole line of *college* crap, right, how goddam sophisticated you are or something, sure, if she won't go down for you she's *bound* to go down

21

for Silas Marner. And who am I, I'm just this dumb shmuck that sells Pontiacs for his old man. (*Clint coughs twice again, louder. Cheryl and Ronda have paused at the far end of the beach, listening to Ricky. They look at one another in amusement.*) Well you know what I think? (*Louder.*) I don't think this girl is even gonna give *you* the time of day! Chicks like her don't have to waste their time with assholes! (*Clint begins coughing steadily, in little bursts of two.*) Chicks like her can take one good look at a guy and tell right away whether or not he's some kind of moron! Just by the way he looks! And once they've made up their mind you're a dork, forget it—you're *never* gonna get in! You might just as well go off somewhere and yank your crank! (*Pause.*) What's the matter with your fucking throat? (*Clint indicates with a furious little gesture. Ricky turns and sees the women staring at him. Slight pause.*) So anyway, that's the way the big speech reads in my new movie. You like it? I told them I thought it was a little overwritten, but Bob said don't change a word, kid, you do it great. That Bob, he's a helluva guy. Good ol' Bob. (*Pause.*) Bob Redford? (*Cheryl and Ronda, holding back laughter, begin to spread out their beach things. During the following Cheryl will put suntan lotion on and Ronda will read a paperback.*)

CLINT. (*To Ricky.*) What was it you said the name of that movie was?

RICKY. The name of that one—?

CLINT. Wasn't it called "The Unbelievable Jerk?"

RICKY. Uh, that's right. That's right, yeah. But they're thinking of changing the title. Jacky's not too happy with that one. (*Pause.*) Jacqueline Bisset?

CLINT. Right.

RICKY. Yeah.

CLINT. Well, hey, I'm really glad you could fly in from the coast. It's been great to see you again.

RICKY. Yeah, good to see you too.

CLINT. How soon do you have to leave?

RICKY. Leave?

CLINT. Don't you have to go back pretty soon? To start the new movie?

RICKY. Oh, that! No, I've got a few days.

CLINT. That wasn't the impression I got from Sid.

RICKY. Sid.

CLINT. Your agent.
RICKY. Oh Sid!
CLINT. Sid, right. He called.
RICKY. When?
CLINT. This morning. Said for you to call him back at lunch-time. (*He looks up at the sun.*) Ooops, almost noon.
RICKY. It can wait.
CLINT. You're not going back to the room to call him?
RICKY. Not right now.
CLINT. He's gonna be mad, if I know Sid.
RICKY. You don't know Sid the way I know Sid.
CLINT. I guess nobody does. (*Silence while the women relax and the men stare at them furtively.*)
RICKY. I could do with a beer.
CLINT. I'm not thirsty.
RICKY. I think we could all do with a beer.
CLINT. No thanks.
RICKY. All.
CLINT. Oh. (*Pause.*) Good idea! I could really do with a beer.
RICKY. Here we go.
CLINT. Whew! Hot out here!
RICKY. (*Addresses women casually.*) Hey, uh—would either of you guys care for a beer? (*Pause.*) It's *Coors.* (*Pause.*) Uh—excuse me—?
RONDA. (*Looking up from her book.*) Were you talking to us?
RICKY. Yeah.
RONDA. I thought I heard you say "you guys."
RICKY. That's right. You guys.
RONDA. That's what had me confused. You said you *guys,* but there aren't any guys here. Except you guys.
RICKY. Yeah, well, it's just an expression.
RONDA. What?
RICKY. You guys.
RONDA. (*To Cheryl.*) There he goes again!
CHERYL. (*Aside, to Ronda.*) What are you *doing?*
RICKY. You know what I mean.
RONDA. (*To Ricky.*) What?
RICKY. What I mean is, I should've said, you girls.
RONDA. Don't call us that.
RICKY. Why not?

23

RONDA. We're women.

RICKY. Oh yeah, right—women's lib, right? I've read that.

RONDA. *Girls* is condescending.

RICKY. Yeah.

RONDA. And sexist.

RICKY. Right. (*Pause.*) That's why I said you *guys.*

RONDA. Well if we're women then how can we be guys? That doesn't make any sense. Just because we don't want to be called girls doesn't mean we *do* want to be called men. Unless maybe we don't look like women at all to you—in which case you should maybe get your eyes checked.

CLINT. (*To Ricky, aside.*) Watch out for your nuts. She's foaming at the mouth.

RICKY. (*To Clint, aside.*) Jesus, do you believe the *pile* she's putting out?

CHERYL. (*To Ronda, aside.*) What is *wrong* with you?

RONDA. (*To Cheryl, aside.*) Don't worry, I can handle these creeps.

CHERYL. You'll scare them off.

RONDA. That's okay, they're not our type.

CHERYL. (*Warningly.*) Ronnie—

RICKY. (*To the women.*) Listen, you guys want a beer or not?

RONDA. It's fattening.

RICKY. It's *Coors.* It's three-fifty a six-pack.

RONDA. Then it's fattening and overpriced.

RICKY. Okay, you're welcome!

RONDA. Thanks anyway. (*Silence while the men return reluctantly to their towels and sunbathe. Ronda returns to her book. Cheryl fans herself, bored. She looks around.*)

CHERYL. (*Pause. Softly.*) I'll have one. (*The men both leap for the cooler, but Ricky gets there first and pulls out a beer. He crosses to Cheryl with it. Clint sits warily on the cooler, watching to see what will happen.*)

RONDA. *Cheryl.*

CHERYL. No, I'd like to taste it. I've never had one of those.

RICKY. It's really good. (*He pops one, hands it to her.*) Made with Rocky Mountain spring water. Paul Newman drinks them.

CHERYL. Oh, do you know him?

RICKY. Paul Newman?

CHERYL. I heard you say you were in movies. I thought possibly you might know him.

CLINT. Paul? Sure, he knows Paul.

RONDA. Ha.

CLINT. Tell them about Paul.

RICKY. We're not really that close. He calls me up once in awhile and asks me to come to one of his stockcar races, but I can't stand the noise.

CHERYL. Are his eyes really as blue as they look in the movies?

RICKY. Sort of a turquoise.

CHERYL. Is his hair really that gray?

RICKY. It's more silver.

RONDA. He sounds like a Navaho bracelet.

CHERYL. Oh, and is he really short? Cause like I've always heard that, but if you say he's really short I'll just be heartbroken.

RICKY. He's kind of.

CHERYL. Oh wow. It must be so exciting to work with all those famous people every day.

RICKY. Yeah, I guess. I don't know. I find a lot of them pretty shallow.

CLINT. (*Rises and crosses to join the others.*) Ricky doesn't like to talk about the business too much while he's on vacation, y'know?

CHERYL. Oh, I'm sorry.

RICKY. (*To Clint.*) No, I don't mind talking about it.

CLINT. He likes to get his mind off it and relax. He just hates it when people recognize him.

RONDA. I'll bet.

RICKY. (*To Cheryl.*) I don't mind the fans coming up to me. They have a right to display their affection.

CLINT. Ricky, these ladies don't want to hear your boring old Hollywood stories. Some other time, maybe.

CHERYL. No, I'd love to hear them.

RICKY. I'd be happy to tell you some more. Privately.

CHERYL. (*Who's having a hard time keeping a straight face.*) Would you? That would be wonderful.

RICKY. I've got lots of 'em.

RONDA. Cheryl . . .

CLINT. Ricky . . .

RICKY. Shut up, Clint baby. (*To Cheryl.*) That's how we talk out in Beverly Hills. Clint baby—key grip—percentage points . . .

25

CLINT. (*To Cheryl.*) You'll have to excuse him, he's getting brain fever. We've been out here all morning.

CHERYL. Are you his manager?

CLINT. Me? No.

RICKY. No.

CLINT. (*To Ricky.*) Absolutely *not.*

RICKY. No, he's my bodyguard. (*Clint looks at him furiously.*)

CHERYL. Really?

RICKY. I guess we haven't met. My name is Ricky, and my bodyguard here is Clint.

CHERYL. I'm Cheryl, and this is my friend Ronnie. Ronda.

RONDA. Just exactly what movies have you been in?

CHERYL. *Ronnie.* That's rude. (*To men.*) You'll have to excuse her, she's weak from dieting.

RONDA. Name one.

RICKY. A movie? I was in?

CLINT. Tell them a movie you were in, Ricky baby.

RICKY. Sure. (*Pause.*) I was in *The Towering Inferno.*

CHERYL. You're kidding!

RICKY. That's where I met Paul and Steverino. Steve McQueen?

CHERYL. Oh wow—were you a faller or a burner?

RICKY. Oh I insisted on burning. It was in my contract.

RONDA. What part did you play?

RICKY. I played—the elevator man.

CHERYL. Oh my God—I remember you!

RICKY. You do? It was just a small part.

CHERYL. Sure I do! How could I ever forget? Oh wow, of course! You did that great *scream,* didn't you? The one where you were flapping your arms at the flames that were all over you?

RICKY. Yeah, I guess I did.

CHERYL. Oh wow, that must've really hurt your throat.

RICKY. It was sore for a couple days, yeah.

CHERYL. Well like—could you do it for me now?

RICKY. (*Pause.*) Do it now—?

CHERYL. Could you do that scream for us, right now? Oh, I *loved* it!

RICKY. Well, I don't know, I—

CHERYL. (*Pouting.*) You won't do it? For me?

RICKY. Well, I . . . (*Clint and Ronda are looking anxiously around at the crowded beach. Ronda starts to quickly pack her* beach bag to leave. Clint stands and tries to hustle Ricky away from Cheryl.)

CLINT. The beach is a little crowded right now, Cheryl.

CHERYL. Oh—and I really had my hopes up!

CLINT. The lifeguards might get a little upset.

CHERYL. It was my favorite thing in the whole movie!

RONDA. Cheryl, people are looking.

CLINT. Ricky baby has to rest his voice for his new flick, so maybe some other time.

CHERYL. (Still in seductive pursuit of Ricky.) You won't do just a little bit—?

RONDA. Cheryl!

CLINT. Ricky—Ricky, don't you dare—

CHERYL. Just for me?

RICKY. Well, if you put it that way . . . (Ricky gestures dramatically for the others to stand back. He looks down at the sand, then pretends to notice flames creeping towards his feet. He backs away in terror.) No . . . No! . . . Noouooooo! (Cheryl watches this entire sequence with excited squeals and applause. Ronda is mortified with embarrassment and keeps staring around to see who's looking. Clint kneels at the cooler and tries to hide his head in it. Ricky has begun slapping at his feet, giving out little horrified yelps. He watches flames race up his body, slapping at them frantically and letting out a succession of blood-curdling screams. He races blindly about, flapping his arms and screaming, and then does an agonized death scene, which involves choking, gasping, falling to the sand, rolling over, and at last a sort of broken crawl towards Cheryl. He ends by "dying" in her lap, to her great delight. He opens his eyes and beams up at her.)

(Blackout.)

Scene Four. Saturday Evening.

The men's motel room. Clint is in shorts, towelling his wet hair. During the course of the scene he will blow-dry his hair, put on aftershave, dress, etc. Ricky is off at the top of the scene, in the bathroom.

27

CLINT. You piece of grunt.

RICKY. (*Off.*) It worked, didn't it?

CLINT. You stinking piece of grunt.

RICKY. (*Off.*) They're going out to dinner, right? So what are you still whacking off about?

CLINT. I can't believe you did that. Steverino? Bodyguard? Jesus!

RICKY. (*Off.*) I thought for a second that lifeguard was gonna kick the crap out of me.

CLINT: I wish he had.

RICKY. (*Off.*) I didn't see you making any great moves.

CLINT. You didn't see me acting like a retard, either.

RICKY. (*Off.*) Somebody had to do something.

CLINT. And you sure as hell did it, Ricky baby.

RICKY. (*Off.*) She *asked* to see my scream. It wasn't my idea.

CLINT. You didn't have to do it so loud! (*Ricky enters, with a towel wrapped around his waist. He is combing his wet hair.*)

RICKY. Just remember one thing, ace. You can't chase pussy in a three-piece suit.

CLINT. (*Pause.*) What the hell is that supposed to mean?

RICKY. It means, I'll make a fool of myself any day of the week for a piece of ass. You gotta be willing to go the distance. That's the thrill of the hunt.

CLINT. Well at least they accepted our invitation. I just hope it's gonna be worth it.

RICKY. Worth it? Didn't you see those hooters?

CLINT. I couldn't help noticing them, yes.

RICKY. A Ten, right?

CLINT. At least.

RICKY. What did I tell you?

CLINT. Okay, you've got eyes. (*Pause.*) What I can't believe is the way they always travel in *teams.* Have you noticed that?

RICKY. Jesus, could you believe that other chick? What a bitch.

CLINT. Two-man teams, like hit men or something. There's always a big good-looking one, and then a little one that couldn't get arrested. I see them all the time at school, dances and stuff. They look like a rhino and that little bird that sits on its back and eats bugs. They sit there with this real take-me look, but they never *dance* with anybody. And every freshman in the joint is just *aching* to snake the one who's a real babe, but whenever you ask her to dance she always says—

RICKY and CLINT. (*Together.*) "No thanks, I'm with my girlfriend."

CLINT. Right! And nobody's *ever* gonna take on the pig, so the foxy one is safe. It's like a defense mechanism.

RICKY. Yeah, you can bet she'd ditch the little one fast enough if she saw somebody she really wanted. But unless she does, she can always come on like she's got this incredible *loyalty* to her friend or something.

CLINT. Yeah. . . . How's my hair look?

RICKY. It's lookin' pretty sharp, ace.

CLINT. Lookin' all right?

RICKY. Uptight.

CLINT. Outasight!

RICKY. You need some aftershave?

CLINT. Whattya got?

RICKY. (*Looking through shaving kit.*) I got *Old Spice, English Leather, Brut*—

CLINT. I like that.

RICKY. Nah, I think we oughtta load for bear. Here we go. (*Takes out a small bottle.*) *Musk Oil.* It's like nerve gas—the chicks are paralyzed.

CLINT. Sounds good to me. (*They put some on.*)

RICKY. So what's your game plan, coach?

CLINT. Well the way I see it, this girl is no dummy. We're not gonna get to first base with her unless we come on smart. Girls like that don't go down for airheads.

RICKY. She's got class.

CLINT. Class to her ass. We're not dealing with a girl who appreciates the caveman approach.

RICKY. Essence of jockstrap?

CLINT. Not her type. No, no, we've gotta come on smart. Mature. Cultured. (*Pause.*) We've gotta come on like Alistair Cooke.

RICKY. Uh, Alistair may be a bit too old for this chick, Clint.

CLINT. You know what I mean. We find an Italian restaurant somewhere. We're dressed to the teeth. Candlelight, wine, music. Dancing is always good, too, gets the old contact started. And everytime we take a break from the dancing, we're going on like crazy about Kurt Vonnegut and Kahlil Gibran, stuff like that. Kill 'em with our sensitivity.

RICKY. I never read those guys.

CLINT. I can tell you everything you need to know in five minutes. Helps if you throw in some women's lib stuff too. Tell 'em you're real worried cause the ERA's in trouble.

RICKY. (*Pause.*) Would you say you've had a pretty good score ratio with this technique?

CLINT. It's dynamite.

RICKY. Talk some numbers. How many?

CLINT. My whole freshman year? Five, six.

RICKY. That means two. And a couple more you felt up, till they found out you were a freshman.

CLINT. Listen, college happens to be a fantastic place to score! You don't even know what you're missing.

RICKY. I'm sure that's true, Clint. But with all due respect, we've got one evening to operate here, not two semesters. So bear in mind that although *my* old man is not blowing several grand to float *me* through four years of summer camp, I *have*, in the course of my travels and in my own humble way, stumbled across one or two points of practical interest. May I?

CLINT. (*Sourly.*) Be my guest, Ricky baby.

RICKY. Point One: Surprise.

CLINT. Surprise.

RICKY. Key element. These chicks think we're all going out to a restaurant, correct?

CLINT. We're not?

RICKY. No way. Picnic. Moonlight. I-so-la-tion.

CLINT. But we invited them to a restaurant! What if they don't accept going on a picnic?

RICKY. You don't give chicks a choice, idiot. You tell them.

CLINT. But what if they won't go?

RICKY. Believe me, they'll go. If there's one thing chicks like more than getting laid, it's eating. We bring along the food and we brush a few odors in their direction.

CLINT. I don't know . . .

RICKY. Okay, now you've caught them off-guard and you're ready for Point Two: Beer. Plenty of it. We serve lots of extra-salty fried seafood, and we make sure there's nothing non-alcoholic to drink. With me so far?

CLINT. Got it.

30

RICKY. Point Three: Talk Dirty.

CLINT. Talk dirty?

RICKY. You know. Keep subtly leading the conversation into areas that are a little off-color. They pretend to be shocked, but actually they find it titillating, and I think that word says it all.

CLINT. Is this what you did all through high school? Developed this system?

RICKY. Point Four: Divide and Conquer.

CLINT. Meaning?

RICKY. Meaning we carve the gargoyle away from the Ten. Deprive her of the natural ally! One of us waves a red flag in front of this Ronda creep while the other goes in for the kill. Matadors use this same technique. So, that's my plan—sound good?

CLINT. Crude, but effective. It might just work.

RICKY. Repeat after me: Point One, Surprise. Point Two, Beer. Point Three, Talk Dirty. Point Four, Divide and Conquer.

CLINT. Surprise, beer, dirty talk, divide and conquer. Okay, I'm willing to try it your way. But it better work.

RICKY. Hey, I wasn't Rick the Stick for nothing. Stick with the Stick and you'll get an education that *means* something.

CLINT. Great, then we're set on our plan of attack.

RICKY. All set on the Ten.

CLINT. Ready to go after the Ten!

RICKY. Great on that Ten!

CLINT. Okay then, buddy! You and me.

RICKY. Okay, ace!

CLINT. Okay! (*Pause.*) There's just one little thing.

RICKY. What's that?

CLINT. (*Pause.*) Which one of us is going to walk the dog?

Sharing   (Blackout.)   *be heard manipulate Control her*

Scene Five. Saturday Evening.

The women's room. They are almost finished dressing to go out. They wear pretty summer dresses, high heels, jewelry, etc. Cheryl smokes, puts on makeup.

RONDA. Where's my bracelet?

CHERYL. I haven't seen it.

31

RONDA. I let you wear it yesterday. You were the last to see it.

CHERYL. I gave it back.

RONDA. You did not.

CHERYL. Yes I did.

RONDA. When?

CHERYL. Last night, when we were unpacking.

RONDA. You better not have lost that bracelet.

CHERYL. Ronnie.

RONDA. If you have I'll murder you. Jerry Potts gave me that bracelet. It's very special.

CHERYL. It must be around here somewhere.

RONDA. I've looked everywhere. It's gone.

CHERYL. Well, you must've put it in with your makeup and your other jewelry. Did you look in here?

RONDA. Of course I looked in there! I'm really not a total moron, thanks a lot.

CHERYL. (*Looking in makeup bag.*) Ronnie, why are you being so hostile?

RONDA. I'm not being hostile. I just want that bracelet you stole.

CHERYL. If you didn't want to go out tonight you could've just said something.

RONDA. Oh sure. I could've said excuse me, but I really think both you guys are total creeps. They wouldn't have even heard me—you were *panting* too loud for normal conversation.

CHERYL. I see. We should've stayed in our room tonight and watched the lightbulb burn out.

RONDA. How in the world you could just stand there and pretend you *believed* that crap about the movies—it was enough to turn my stomach!

CHERYL. Ronnie, it was fun! Didn't you think it was fun to let those two kids think they could impress us into going out to dinner?

RONDA. But we *are* going out to dinner!

CHERYL. So?

RONDA. So who's so smart?

CHERYL. When he started talking about Paul Newman it was all I could do to keep a straight face. And when he did that scream—? (*Imitates Ricky's expression and arm-flapping.*) Could you just die? (*She laughs.*)

RONDA. Great logic. He can throw a spastic fit on a public

beach, so he must be a good date. What does he have to do to be the father of your children—dribble down the side of his chin?

CHERYL. I think you're getting a little carried away here. It's just a dinner date.

RONDA. Terrific. And who do I get, the bodyguard?

CHERYL. I think he's cute too.

RONDA. Great. Remind me to go down on him under the table.

CHERYL. I don't know how you can be so cynical. Don't you ever just want to have a good time?

RONDA. A quickie on Cape Cod with a couple of jerky strangers is not my idea of a good time.

CHERYL. Who said anything about a quickie?

RONDA. Oh don't tell me the thought hadn't occurred to you.

CHERYL. Ron, they're kids!

RONDA. Don't tell me it hasn't occurred to them.

CHERYL. Of course it has. It's the only thought their little heads are capable of holding at one time. That's the fun part.

RONDA. Fun part?

CHERYL. Leading them by the nose.

RONDA. Or whatever else is straight and sticks out.

CHERYL. Sure!

RONDA. You're not back in junior high, even if you act like it.

CHERYL. And you're not the principal, even though you talk like him.

RONDA. You make me sound like some kind of prude.

CHERYL. You are.

RONDA. I've slept with men!

CHERYL. Two.

RONDA. Three!

CHERYL. Well. Two and a half.

RONDA. (Angrily.) You leave Jerry Potts out of this! He's suffered enough.

CHERYL. I didn't say anything.

RONDA. Anyway it doesn't matter who I've slept with. It's not something you keep a scorecard in!

CHERYL. Of course not.

RONDA. Even though you think it is.

CHERYL. I do not!

RONDA. I don't know how you could do this to David. You're practically engaged to him.

CHERYL. Oh-Ho! Now it's David.

RONDA. I think this is just a crude attempt to score points on him in some kind of dumb game you've made up. I'd ask myself what I was after if I was you.

CHERYL. *David* wants me to feel middleaged. David wants me to be the mother of three in a ranch wagon on my way to the PTA! Well forget that.

RONDA. Try your real age.

CHERYL. Oh, okay, what's that? How are you supposed to act when you're 25? You tell me, you're the expert—does it mean you're still allowed to have fun, but not quite as much? Or you can *have* it, but you can't let it show?

RONDA. Being a kid and acting immature are not the same thing.

CHERYL. (*Pause.*) You know what you are, Ron? You're a conscientious objector. When the trumpets sounded for the sexual revolution, I think you just charged in the opposite direction.

RONDA. Maybe I just refused to be drafted!

CHERYL. Well you can relax now, the revolution's over. This is just a mopping-up operation.

RONDA. (*Very upset.*) I hate it! I hate being so *free* that I'm *compelled* to do something I never asked for the freedom to do in the first place! I never *asked* for it, so thanks a lot! And something that somebody as pretty as you could've always done anyway. Well where does that leave me if I don't want to? Where does that leave *me?*

CHERYL. (*Pause.*) You really are getting very worked up over a crummy little seafood dinner. A couple shrimp and a lousy clam roll? (*She laughs.*)

RONDA. Where's my bracelet?

CHERYL. Ron, talk to me.

RONDA. If I'm going to have zits all over my face from seafood, I can at least wear something shiny. Maybe it'll distract them.

CHERYL. You're really mad at me, aren't you?

RONDA. (*Pause.*) I thought I came to the beach to be with you. I thought you wanted to get *away* from guys for one weekend, and we'd talk. Maybe get some sun, and talk things out. (*Pause.*) This isn't fair, Cheryl.

CHERYL. I'm sorry, Ron. (*Pause.*) I guess I got a little carried away here. (*Pause.*) Listen. We'll have a couple drinks, we'll eat, we'll say goodnight and come home together. Alone. Okay?

RONDA. Do you mean it?

CHERYL. Yes.

RONDA. But do you really mean it?

CHERYL. I promise.

RONDA. (*Pause.*) Okay.

CHERYL. Okay. (*Ronda runs to Cheryl, hugs her impulsively. The doorbell rings.*)

RONDA. Oh God it's them. The epileptic and his bodyguard. Cher, what am I going to do?

CHERYL. Get the door.

RONDA. Right. (*Ronda goes off to answer the door. Cheryl smoothes her clothes. Ronda returns with Clint and Ricky, who wear beach gear—jeans, shirts, windbreakers, Ricky carries a large picnic basket and a blanket. Clint struggles with the cooler, now very heavy. The men are tensely cheerful; open warfare is just below the surface.*)

RICKY. Hey hey hey!

CLINT. Whattya say?

RONDA. Go a-way.

RICKY. Pardon?

RONDA. Did I say something?

CHERYL. What's all this?

RICKY. *This*—is dinner.

CLINT. And this is liquid refreshment. Whew! Long way from the parking lot. (*He drops the cooler on a bed.*)

RICKY. We had to drive all the way into town to get this stuff. Cost us an arm and a leg.

CLINT. Guy wouldn't even let us rent the basket.

RICKY. Had to flat out *buy* the damned thing.

CLINT. No problem, though.

RICKY. No problem. Care for a starter? (*Offers a beer to Cheryl.*)

CHERYL. Wait a minute! What happened to dinner out? I thought there was this great place you guys knew.

CLINT. Uh, that place was closed.

RONDA. Closed?

CLINT. Yeah, health inspection. Lost their license.

RICKY. What he means is, we thought it would be a lot more fun, since none of us gets to the beach that often, and since it's such a nice night, maybe you guys—I'm sorry—maybe you ladies—

CLINT. Women.

RICKY. Probably you women would like to eat outside.

CLINT. Fresh air.

RICKY. Salty breezes.

RONDA. You mean there's no restaurant with outdoor dining?

RICKY. Well—this way we pick our own view.

CLINT. Anyway, we already bought all the food, so we're not asking you—we're telling you.

RICKY. What he *means* is, we thought it'd be fun, and we've gone to a bit of bother, but hey—absolutely up to you guys.

CLINT. Women.

CHERYL. Just a minute. (*Cheryl takes Ronda off to one side to talk. Ricky pulls Clint to the other end of the room.*)

RICKY. Asshole! Do you hear yourself?

CLINT. Shut up!

RICKY. Will you let me lead? Will you stick to the plan?

CLINT. I'm allowed to have a few ideas.

CHERYL. (*To Ronda.*) What do you think?

RONDA. Is this the most obvious thing you ever saw, or what?

CHERYL. It's up to you. Should we bag it right now?

RICKY. (*To Clint.*) It's *my* plan—you'll screw up everything!

CLINT. Well from now on, it's every man for himself!

RICKY. (*To the women, sweetly.*) Take your time!

CHERYL. Okay!

RONDA (*To Cheryl.*) Look at them. They're even more harmless than I thought.

CHERYL. Shall we?

RONDA. Oh, why not? I'm starving.

CHERYL. You might even have fun. Pretend to go along with them. (*Ronda nods. Cheryl turns to the men, who are still arguing quietly with each other.*) Okay, let's go.

RICKY. (*Startled.*) What?

CHERYL. We'll do it.

CLINT. You will?

RONDA. The sooner we eat, the sooner we'll get home, right?

RICKY. . . . Right.

RONDA. Then let's go.

CHERYL. Let's go!

RICKY. You heard the ladies, Clint. Let's go!

CLINT. Women, Richard. Women. (*The men pick up the picnic*

36

supplies and follow the women out onto the boardwalk. They all walk slowly to the beach area, D. where they will look for a place to eat.)

RONDA. What kinda stuff did you bring?

RICKY. Oh, you name it. We got fried chicken, we got shrimp, corn on the cob—

CLINT. Cole slaw, potato salad—

RICKY. French fries, onion rings— *(To Cheryl.)* You like rings?

CHERYL. Crazy about 'em.

RONDA. Oh me too. I love greasy food.

CHERYL. Ronnie . . .

RONDA. Okay. *(Clint is swaying from the weight of the cooler, and has to pause on the boardwalk to catch his breath. During the following Ricky keeps up with the women, while Clint is always well behind and out of breath.)*

RICKY. Let's get a move on with that cooler, Clint.

CLINT. I'm coming, I'm coming!

CHERYL. Gosh, how much beer is in there?

RICKY. I'm trying to build up his muscle tone.

CLINT. This looks like a good spot. What's wrong with right here?

RICKY. Let's let the women decide, shall we Clint? What do you say, Cher?

CHERYL. I don't know . . . Ron?

RONDA. Mmmm . . . maybe over here.

CHERYL. Here?

RICKY. Anywhere you say. C'mon, Clint. *(Clint crosses with cooler to where they're standing, but by the time he arrives they're already moving away.)*

RONDA. No . . . no, that's no good. Maybe over this way . . .

CHERYL. You guys don't mind, do you?

RICKY. Hey, no problem!

RONDA. I just can't decide.

RICKY. Take your time. Where you go, we go. *(With a huge effort Clint staggers to where they now stand.)*

CLINT. I love this spot.

RONDA. *(Pause.)* No . . . I think I was right the first time. That was definitely the best spot back over there.

CHERYL. It was more level.

37

RONDA: Yeah, over here. (*The women cross back to a spot near* c., *with Ricky following.*)
CHERYL. (*To Ricky.*) Is this okay with you guys?
RICKY. Looks fine to me. Clint, just set the cooler down over there if you would. (*Clint drops the cooler in the indicated spot and collapses on it, out of breath.*)
RONDA. You need some help setting up?
CHERYL. What can we do?
RICKY. Oh hey—we'll take care of that. You guys just stand over here and work up a thirst, cause there's plenty of brew. Clint, for Pete's sake, don't just *sit* there—offer these women a beer.
CLINT. (*Cranky.*) I'll let you do that, Richard. You're the expert, since you get it from Paul Newman. (*Ricky puts down the basket, crosses to cooler. He throws the blanket to Clint.*)
RICKY. Fine, *J'll* get the beer. You spread out the blanket.
CHERYL. Oh, you guys thought of everything! Look, Ron, they brought a blanket.
CLINT. I'm the one who thought of this.
CHERYL. That was sweet.
CLINT. Yeah, I didn't want you to get your clothes messed up.
RICKY. Well stop yakking and spread it *out*, Clint. (*He crosses back with beers for the women.*) Here you go—drink up. Let me open this for you, Cher. You like this beer?
CHERYL. Is this what I had this afternoon? Cause if they're heavy they go right to my head. (*Clint spreads out the blanket.*)
RICKY. Oh no, this beer's real light. You could drink a million of these and not feel a thing.
CLINT. Excuse me, Rick—am I in your way here?
RICKY. No, I'm fine,
CLINT. I'm not getting in your way doing all the work, am I?
RICKY. (*To Cheryl.*) Will you excuse me for a sec while I give Clint a hand?
CHERYL. Sure. (*Ricky gets plates and plastic forks and spoons from basket. He and Clint set these out on the blanket.*)
RONDA. (*To Ricky.*) Tell us some more about Paul Newman.
RICKY. Oh, there's not much to tell.
CLINT. I'll say.
CHERYL. There must be some little story you could tell us.
RONDA. We'd love to hear it.
CLINT. Yeah, Rick, we'd love to hear it.

RICKY. I'll tell you later. Right now I'm starving.
RONDA. Promise you will?
RICKY. Sure, sure.
RONDA. Okay, I'm gonna hold you to it.
CHERYL. Me too.
CLINT. Me three.
RICKY. Drink up, ladies, we'll only be a minute here.
CLINT. Women, Richard. (*Ricky crosses back to cooler, gets two more beers for the women. He hands these to them even though they're still holding their old ones.*)
RICKY. Here you go. And there's plenty more where that came from.
RONDA. How much did all this cost?
RICKY. Well, you know what they say about beer.
CHERYL. No, what do they say?
RICKY. "You can't buy beer—you can only rent it."
CLINT. Hilarious, Rick. What does that have to do with anything?
RICKY. I was *talking* to Cheryl here, Clint baby.
CLINT. I *noticed* that. Maybe you'd like to give me a hand here instead.
RICKY. Drink up—I'll just be a second. (*Ricky crosses to basket. During the following he throws containers of food to Clint, who places them on the blanket.*)
CHERYL. Is something wrong?
RICKY. Wrong? What could be wrong? (*Throwing at Clint.*) Clams.
CLINT. Clams!
RONDA. Are you guys fighting, or what?
RICKY. Fighting? Nah! We kid each other all the time. (*Throwing.*) Shrimp!
CLINT. Yeah, we're great old kidders.
RICKY. Great ones. (*Throwing.*) Cole slaw!
CLINT. But sometimes we go too far.
RICKY. (*Throwing.*) Potato Salad! Pickles! French fries!
CLINT. And then later we're really sorry.
RICKY. And of course, last but not least . . . (*Ricky pulls a floral arrangement out of the basket, sets it on the blanket with a flourish. The women applaud, Ricky bows.*)
CHERYL. Oh, this is wonderful!
RONDA. Very nice.

RICKY. (*Motions for them to sit.*) Shall we? (*Women cross to sit. There is a brief flurry of movement as both men try to sit next to Cheryl, but when the women also switch positions Clint ends up sitting next to Ronda, and Ricky next to Cheryl. They all sit.*)

CHERYL. You guys shouldn't have gone to all this trouble.

RICKY. Listen, it was no trouble. Eat all you want, there's plenty of food.

CHERYL. These clams look pretty good.

RONDA. The shrimps too. Could I have some of those?

CLINT. Sure, here you go.

RONDA. Cher, you want some of these?

CHERYL. I'll get started on the clams.

RONDA. Okay. (*The women eat, while the men watch anxiously. Women slowly react to strange taste of food.*)

CHERYL. Hmmm . . .

RONDA. I think maybe there's something wrong with these shrimp.

CHERYL. The clams too. Taste this. (*Hands a bite to Ronda.*)

RONDA. They're incredibly salty. . . .

CLINT. Are they?

RICKY. Let me try one of those. (*Tastes.*) Gosh, you're right.

RONDA. Tastes like somebody dumped an entire shaker of salt over them.

CLINT. God, and we told the guy to go *easy* on it.

RICKY. You can't get decent service in these fast-food places.

CHERYL. Well—I guess we could just sort of brush them off. . . .

CLINT. Sure, that's an idea.

RICKY. Guess we'll just have to make the best of it.

RONDA. These shrimp are turning my mouth inside out! Could I have some of that cole slaw?

CLINT. Here you go. And here's some for you, Cheryl.

CHERYL. God, is this stuff ever making me *thirsty!*

RICKY. Well, there's nothing like a cold beer to solve that little problem. I'll just get us some more. (*He crosses to cooler.*)

RONDA. I don't believe it! Who ever heard of salty cole slaw?

CHERYL. Maybe you could wipe it with a napkin or something. Here.

RONDA. I'll try. I've got to eat *something.*

RICKY. (*Returning with two six-packs.*) This ought to help.

CHERYL. Oh God, give me one of those.

RICKY. Sure, here you go. Drink up, gang! (*They drink, Cheryl taking a longer swallow than anyone else.*) Clint, you take it easy, though. You know how you were always a two beer man in high school.

CHERYL. Clint! Is that true?

RICKY. Oh yeah, two cans and he'd blow lunch in the back seat of my car. We'd be double dating or something—we were always in my car—you know, even today Clint doesn't have his own—and we'd be driving along and all of a sudden you'd hear old Clint ralphing away in the back seat. Clint the Splint we called him then.

CHERYL. Oh, that's so sad.

RONDA. I hated the taste of beer in high school.

CHERYL. Me too, cause it made me dizzy. But I always had to force myself to drink it so the other cheerleaders wouldn't think I was stuck up.

CLINT. Oh, were you a cheerleader? So was my sister.

CHERYL. Mmm, I was head cheerleader.

RICKY. I'll bet you were.

CHERYL. As a junior.

CLINT. God, that was quite an honor. Of course if you were half as pretty then as you are now, they really didn't have much choice.

CHERYL. Oh, it was on school spirit and all kinds of stuff.

RICKY. But you had all those things too, didn't you?

CHERYL. Oh sure.

RONDA. This beer's good.

CLINT. Yeah.

CHERYL. It's nice and cold.

RICKY. Yeah.

CHERYL. Cheers! (*They all drink, Cheryl again taking a longer swallow than anyone else. Ricky is amazed at her capacity.*)

RICKY. Hey, Cher, you're quite a chugger.

CHERYL. Thanks. I bet you're pretty good too.

RICKY. Tell you what—let's you and me go one on one. Whattya say?

CHERYL. You're on. (*He hands her a fresh beer.*)

RICKY. Ready? One—two—three—go! (*They chug the beers. Ricky manages to lose. Cheryl finishes first and tosses her empty can over her shoulder.*)

CHERYL. I won!

41

RICKY. Oh God. I'm out of shape! You're too much. You gotta give me another chance.

CLINT. Hey, everybody, look at that sunset!

RONDA. Very nice.

CLINT. Spectacular.

CHERYL. I'm glad you guys had the idea of eating outside. This is fun. (*She reaches for another beer.*)

RICKY. Sure is.

CLINT. You know—this sunset reminds me of a passage from *The Prophet.* By Kahlil Gibran? "Your children are arrows, shot from a bow and arrow towards the sun. You do not know the target . . . only the string." Something like that.

CHERYL. I think it's "You only bend the bow."

RONDA. And then let go.

CHERYL. Yeah! Oh God, I haven't thought about that book for years! (*Laughs.*) Seems completely ridiculous now, doesn't it?

CLINT. (*A bit crestfallen.*) Yeah.

RICKY. *Yeah.*

CHERYL. You okay, Ron?

RONDA. Fine. It's gonna get chilly out here pretty soon, though.

CHERYL. That's true. I can already feel it a little.

RONDA. We don't want to hang around *too* late.

CHERYL. Maybe we should've brought sweaters.

RICKY. You want one of us to go up to your room and get them?

CHERYL. No, that's okay.

RICKY. Clint could go. Only take a second.

CHERYL. No, I'm fine.

RICKY. Run on up, Clint.

CLINT. (*To Cheryl.*) If you want me to, I will.

CHERYL. Don't bother.

CLINT. Or I could give you my windbreaker.

CHERYL. That might be nice—would you mind?

CLINT. No problem. (*Slips it off and puts it around her, smirking at Ricky.*)

CHERYL. Thanks. Ricky—be sweet and give Ron your windbreaker.

RICKY. If you say so.

RONDA. (*To Ricky.*) Keep it. (*To Cheryl.*) I think maybe we should go up in a little bit.

CHERYL. We just got here.

RONDA. I know, but . . .

CHERYL. Aw—a few more minutes?

RONDA. Okay.

CHERYL. Sure you don't want his windbreaker?

RONDA. No, that's okay.

RICKY. Anything else you need, Cher, you just say the word. You want some more cole slaw?

CHERYL. Maybe a little.

RICKY. It's pretty good.

CLINT. (*To Cheryl.*) Did you ever read *Cat's Cradle*, by Kurt Vonnegut, Jr.?

CHERYL. Oh God, I loved that book!

CLINT. Outasight.

CHERYL. Heinlein was always the best, though.

CLINT. Robert A. Heinlein, sure! *Stranger in a Strange Land*, by Robert A. Heinlein.

CHERYL. My Bible! Did you use to go around trying to grok all your friends?

RICKY. Beg your pardon?

CLINT. I did! I grokked till I was blue in the face.

CHERYL. Maybe we should give it a try. Ron?

RONDA. Oh for pete's sake.

CHERYL. You want to grok us, or should we grok you?

RONDA. This is really too much.

CLINT. You grok me.

CHERYL. Okay. C'mon Ron. (*To Clint.*) Let us know when you're receiving. (*Cheryl groks Clint—which is to say, squeezes her face in concentration close to his and makes weird sounds until he responds with other noises, and both crack up.*)

RICKY. (*Interrupting their laughter, a bit desperately.*) Hey everybody! I hear the EAR is in trouble.

RONDA. The what?

RICKY. The EAR. (*Cheryl and Clint laugh even harder.*) What's so funny?

RONDA. You mean the ERA?

RICKY. Yeah, whatever. Isn't it in trouble?

RONDA. What's it to you?

RICKY. It's too bad, that's all.

RONDA. Women all over America will sleep more soundly tonight, knowing someone cares.

RICKY. I just like to keep in touch with the issues.

RONDA. Sure. You know *why* it's in trouble?

RICKY. Sure.

RONDA. Why?

RICKY. Because.

RONDA. That's right. Because of morons like you.

CHERYL. Ronda!

RONDA. C'mon, Cher, we're going.

CHERYL. You're not even trying!

RONDA. I changed my mind.

CHERYL. Oh, don't make us go now. *Relax*—loosen up. Here, eat some more food.

RONDA. It's too salty.

RICKY. Then drink some more beer, Ron-ron.

RONDA. Why don't you do *The Towering Inferno* again? We're still waiting.

RICKY. Why don't you take a hike?

CHERYL. (*To Ricky.*) Hey, cut it out.

CLINT. Ricky's a little tense. The studio cancelled his three-picture deal.

RICKY. Was that before or after they fired you as my bodyguard?

RONDA. Cheryl, how long are you going to play with these cretins?

RICKY. Cretins?

CHERYL. Stop it, Ronda. You're making something out of nothing. You always do that.

RONDA. Just how long?

CHERYL. I don't know!

RONDA. I think you've been here long enough.

CHERYL. Don't tell me what to do.

RONDA. Well I am telling you. God knows you need somebody to.

CHERYL. Since when did you turn into David?

RONDA. Since you turned back into a cheerleader.

CLINT. Head cheerleader.

CHERYL. (*To Ronda.*) That's right, Ronda. *Head* cheerleader.

RICKY. That's the one in charge of all the other cheerleaders.

CLINT. Here, Cher—have another beer.

CHERYL. Thanks, Clint. (*Takes it, kisses him lightly on cheek.*)

RONDA. (*Reaching.*) I think you've had enough beer too, don't you?

44

CHERYL. I'll let you know when I've had enough.

CLINT. Hey, I never got kissed by a cheerleader before.

RICKY. Me neither.

CHERYL. Head cheerleader.

CLINT. That's right.

RICKY. Me neither, Cheryl.

CHERYL. (*To Clint.*) Did you like it?

CLINT. Sure.

CHERYL. (*Kisses him lightly again, but on the mouth.*) You're sweet.

CLINT. You too. In fact . . . (*He leans over, whispers something to her. She shrieks and slaps at him playfully. They laugh.*)

RICKY. (*Breaking in.*) You know, that's an interesting thing, Cheryl, that term *head.* It's an interesting thing in our language how an ordinary word like that will somehow cross over and take on a whole new meaning. I mean, head cheerleader is one thing, but like you take the exact same word and you add a verb and you get the term "give head." See what I mean? Whole new meaning. (*They stare at him, startled.*) Now let's see—what would be some more of those?

RONDA. Christ.

CLINT. "Jerkoff" is a good one. That can be either a verb or a noun.

RONDA. Or in this case, a plural noun.

CHERYL. (*To Ricky.*) Wait a minute—I'm not quite sure what you're getting at here. (*Teasing.*) You mean like lay? Lay something?

RICKY. Sure. Lay down the book. Lay down the apple. Or the apple gets laid down.

CHERYL. Or lay a person?

RICKY. Lay a person, sure! That counts!

RONDA. (*To Cheryl.*) Give me that beer can.

CHERYL. Stop it. (*To Ricky.*) I see what you mean. Let's see—what's another one?

RICKY. What could be another one?

CHERYL. Oh I know—how about eat it?!

CLINT. Sure! Eat a thing.

RICKY. Eat an orange.

CLINT. Eat that apple you *laid* down.

RICKY. No, you eat it.

CLINT. Why don't you, bigshot?

RICKY. Oh, there's a million. Eat this, eat that, eat them—

CHERYL. Eat my snatch. (*Clint chokes on a mouthful of beer.*)

RICKY. Eat my snatch, sure, that's another one! See how all these words jump around and have different meanings?

CHERYL. This is fun! Let's see—there must be some more with snatch. Ron, what would be some more?

RONDA. Stop it. Just stop it.

CHERYL. Oh! You won't play?

RONDA. No.

CHERYL. Awww. (*Sings, teasing.*) Ev'ry party has a pooper, that's what we invited you-fer— (*The men join in.*) Par-ty poo-per! Par-ty poo-per! (*She stops the singing with a wave.*) Okay, okay, where were we?

RICKY. On snatch.

CHERYL. Purse snatcher!

RICKY. That's a good one.

CLINT. Or snatch a lunch break!

CHERYL. Not so hot. (*She rises, crosses unsteadily to the cooler.*)

RICKY. (*To Clint.*) Hear that? Not so hot.

CLINT. Get bent.

RICKY. Get bent yourself!

CHERYL. What's another one?

RONDA. (*Crossing to Cheryl.*) Cheryl, God damn it!

CHERYL. Hush, Ron, I'm trying to think . . . (*She takes out a beer.*)

RONDA. I'm not leaving you alone here with them.

CHERYL. (*Pushing her aside, absently.*) In a minute . . . I've got it!

RICKY. What?

CHERYL. Bush!

CLINT and RICKY. (*Together.*) Bush!

RICKY. Bush, sure.

CHERYL. (*Crossing back to them.*) All around the mulberry bush!

RICKY. The burning bush!

CLINT. Or I'm really bushed.

RICKY. Or Clint is very bush league.

CLINT. Or how'd you like a knuckle sandwich, behind the bushes?

RICKY. (*To Cheryl.*) Going behind the bushes, sure!

CHERYL. (*Shrieks.*) *Anheuser Busch!*

CLINT. What?

46

CHERYL. (*Pointing to beer can.*) Right here on this label—
Anheuser Busch!

CLINT. Sure, *Anheuser Busch!*

RICKY. (*Pulling Cheryl down by the arm.*) And how's yours,
baby, if you don't mind me asking? (*Cheryl tumbles over the two
of them, all three laughing giddily. Ronda steps in to tug at
Cheryl's arm.*)

RONDA. That's it, you're leaving!

CHERYL. (*Slaps at Ronda's leg, pushes her away.*) Quit, Ronnie!
Honestly! (*To the men.*) Let's see, what are some more? Quick!

CLINT. Cock! How about cock?

RICKY. Sure, there's a good one.

CLINT. There's a great one!

CHERYL. Cockfight!

CLINT. Cocktail.

CHERYL. Cocked hat!

CLINT. Cockatoo!

RICKY. Cock-a-doodle-doo!

CLINT. (*To Ricky.*) How about half-cocked, huh? Half-cocked?

RICKY. More cocked than yours, asshole!

CHERYL. Or dong!

CLINT. Dong, sure!

RICKY. Dong-a-roonies!

CLINT. Dong dong dong!

CHERYL. Ding dong! Ding dong!

CLINT. Who's there?

CHERYL. Howl!

RICKY. Howl?

CLINT. Howl who?

CHERYL. Howl long—is your dong?

CLINT. How long is your dong?!

RICKY. What a riot! (*All three laugh hysterically.*)

RONDA. (*Interrupting furiously.*) I've got one for you—hey!
I've got a great old highschool word for you, Cheryl.

CHERYL. (*Still laughing.*) What's that, Ronda?

RONDA. Twat! (*They are startled into momentary silence.*)
Twat the hell happened to your promise?! (*They stare at her,
amazed.*)

(*Blackout.*)

END OF ACT ONE

ACT TWO

Scene One. Saturday Night.

The beach. Bright moonlight. Surf.

We see the wreckage of the picnic. Ronda is looking through the wadded wrapping paper in the basket. Ricky is sprawled some distance away, beside the cooler. He is sipping a fresh beer, and a small pile of empties has been neatly stacked beside him. Clint and Cheryl are nowhere in sight.

Ricky watches Ronda in silence for a few moments.

RICKY. May I ask you something?
RONDA. Sure love.
RICKY. What are you doing?
RONDA. What does it look like I'm doing?
RICKY. Rooting through the garbage, precious heart.
RONDA. It's called looking for something to eat.
RICKY. Don't you ever do anything besides eat?
RONDA. I *haven't* eaten yet. I'm still starving.
RICKY. No? What was dinner? What was that whole picnic I sat through, just a wonderful dream?
RONDA. Every single thing you brought was inedible. Honey.
RICKY. You're a real winner, you know that?
RONDA. Likewise! (*Silence.*)
RICKY. I don't *have* to sit here, you know. I don't have to sit around out here, if you really want to know the truth, just to watch you stuff your face.
RONDA. Don't do me any favors.
RICKY. I could drive off somewhere and get a burger or something. Play some miniature golf. Hang out.
RONDA. So drive! Golf! Hang, by all means! (*Silence.*)
RICKY. I *would* leave you here too, except I can't, because there's somebody I need to kill.

RONDA. With any luck you'll kill each other. I wouldn't want to miss that.

RICKY. That little asshole! How could he do this to me?

RONDA. Hey? (*Waves her arms.*) Hello? I'm out here too, you know. I'm the one who got stuck with your charming company.

RICKY. I don't even believe he could do this to me.

RONDA. What's to believe?

RICKY. It was my fucking plan!

RONDA. Well it's my fucking room they're in! Fucking!

RICKY. Don't remind me.

RONDA. Where am I supposed to sleep?

RICKY. Ask me if I care! (*Pause.*) I just don't believe this . . .

RONDA. I don't want to hear it again.

RICKY. You wait and wait—

RONDA. I said, I don't want to hear it!

RICKY. (*Pause.*) A weekend it's not raining, not too hot, not too crowded, not too—

RONDA. Shut up! (*She throws a plastic container at him, narrowly missing.*)

RICKY. Hey!

RONDA. What was that? That felt heavy!

RICKY. You vicious little—

RONDA. (*Stands.*) Give that back.

RICKY. (*Picks up container.*) No.

RONDA. (*Crossing to him.*) Give me that!

RICKY. No! You threw it at me. Anyway, I paid for it, whatever it is. (*Opens it.*) It's potato salad. (*Touches a finger to it, licks.*) No salt.

RONDA. (*Reaching.*) Give it to me.

RICKY. Get your hands off! I'll eat it.

RONDA. You're not hungry!

RICKY. I am now.

RONDA. You give me that! It's not fair!

RICKY. No, it's mine. (*She lunges. He pulls the container out of her reach and she falls against him. They wrestle and fall to the ground, then roll over it, fighting for the container.*)

RONDA. Don't drop it!

RICKY. Look out!

RONDA. You'll get sand in it! (*He manages to shove her violently away. She comes back at him, and he shoves her again. She slaps him, hard. He stares at her, astonished. Then he deliberately turns the opened container upside down and shoves it face-first into the sand. When she sees this, she bursts into tears of frustration and rage. He rises, watches her cry for a few moments, very uncomfortable.)*

RICKY. Jesus, all right! Take it, if it means so much to you. Here, I'm not hungry anymore.

RONDA. I hate you!

RICKY. Fine, good.

RONDA. I hate your lousy guts!

RICKY. Right, will you just take the potato salad?

RONDA. I don't want it anymore.

RICKY. You can pick the sand right off it. See? Here, I'll get you started.

RONDA. I wouldn't eat potato salad from you if it was the last potato salad in the world!

RICKY. Well it's not the last potato salad in the world, but it's the last potato salad on this beach and I wish you'd just eat it and shut off the goddam waterworks, okay? *(He crosses cautiously, puts it down beside her.)* I'm putting it down, okay? Right here beside you. Just a little sand on it, comes right off. . . . You'll eat it when you're hungry again. Jeez . . . *(He crosses back to his cooler, sits, takes out another beer and sips. During the following her crying abates, and she picks up the container. She brushes off the sand as best she can and eats.)* I bought a new shirt for this weekend, believe that? Look at it, it's torn, it's got crud all over it . . . all for this lousy weekend. *(Pause.)* You get a new shirt, you get Saturday off—which believe me, if you work for my old man is no picnic even if he is your old man. *(Pause.)* And you call up your former asshole best friend, even though you've hardly seen the stuckup sonofabitch all summer long since he got back from school, but hey—maybe he forgot your phone number! *(With rising anger.)* And you collect this asshole, and you cart him all the way up to Cape fucking Cod, *show* him this unbelievably great-looking chick, and *you* make the first move on her, *you* get her interested, you lay out your entire plan whereby you're going to make this chick, and then this. This! How does this make me feel?

RONDA. If that's supposed to be some kind of apology you'll have to do one hell of a lot better.

50

RICKY. I don't apologize to you! You clear on that? I don't owe you one goddam thing. (*Pause.*) I blame a lot of this on you, you know.

RONDA. On me?!

RICKY. On you, on you!

RONDA. How is that?

RICKY. She's your friend, you should teach her better manners.

RONDA. Since when is my friend my fault? I don't see you doing such a great job with your own lousy friend.

RICKY. That's different. I was betrayed.

RONDA. What was I? (*Furious.*) You think I would've even come here if it'd been my own idea? I came because she needed somebody to talk to. And then look what she does to me! And the worst thing is, the thing that makes me feel the dumbest, is that I *knew* she would. I swear to God, I think sometimes she can't even help herself! And you two! I sit here on this beach and I'm just some piece of driftwood or something, you're both talking over me, around me, through me—well I'd *rather* be betrayed! At least then somebody knows I'm breathing.

RICKY. (*Pause.*) You could've done *something* to make her stay.

RONDA. Did you even hear what I just said?

RICKY. Yeah, but you should've done something. (*Pause.*) How's your potato salad?

RONDA. Crunchy.

RICKY. Great. Wanna beer?

RONDA. Do you always drink like this?

RICKY. Like what?

RONDA. Into an alcoholic stupor?

RICKY. Whenever I get the chance.

RONDA. Charming.

RICKY. Jesus, you always gotta be such a hardass all the time?

RONDA. Have another one, little fella. You're still coherent.

RICKY. Don't you worry about my drinking, angel-drawers. I've drunk more beer than you ever saw.

RONDA. I'm sure you have.

RICKY. I've drunk more beer than you ever *heard* of.

RONDA. Land sakes.

RICKY. I can drink four quarts in one sitting—five!

RONDA. That must be quite a sight. You and Paul Newman in a chugging contest.

RICKY. Aw, just shut the hell up about Paul Newman, okay?

RONDA. Oh, I'm sorry. You probably thought we *believed* all that crap.

RICKY. (*Pause.*) I knew you didn't believe it. That was all part of the plan.

RONDA. Oh, I see.

RICKY. Chicks don't mind whether you're somebody important, long as you *act* like you are. Either get 'em impressed, or get 'em feeling sorry for you. Either way is good.

RONDA. Just make up some lie?

RICKY. Sure! The bigger the better. I once told this one chick I was about to become a priest, and she owed it to Jesus to test my spiritual purity one last time, see was I *worthy* or something.

RONDA. Sad to say, you flunked her test.

RICKY. Sad to say. But that's always a good one with dago chicks, you spot a crucifix or something. Or make it really outrageous. Like you were recently in this three-car pileup in the last lap of the Monaco Grand Prix and you've been paralyzed from the waist down for three months. You've just now got out of intensive care and you're starting to wonder whether you can still be a real man, only you haven't met a chick you thought would really understand and not laugh at you.

RONDA. Up till now, that is.

RICKY. See, you're catching on!

RONDA. And they actually *believe* this nonsense?

RICKY. Believe, what's to believe? Let me tell you something, and you hang onto this as you go through life, because it's God's truth. People will believe what they want to believe, and chicks are no different.

RONDA. But what happens when they don't see any scars on your body?

RICKY. They'll *imagine* them. Whatever! They *want* to believe it, that's the point. If they don't they're still impressed you'd go to all that trouble to bullshit them. Makes them feel really wanted. You know, bullshit is the sincerest form of flattery.

RONDA. Aren't you a little worried about admitting all these top secrets to the enemy?

RICKY. What, to you? What difference does it make?

RONDA. (*She is stung; there's a pause.*) You've really done all this stuff?

RICKY. Plenty of times.

RONDA. You're lying.

RICKY. I have!

RONDA. I don't believe you.

RICKY. So don't believe me. What the hey.

RONDA. I think you talk big.

RICKY. Screw you.

RONDA. I think you're scared.

RICKY. Of you?

RONDA. Of women.

RICKY. *Scared* of women?

RONDA. Yeah!

RICKY. No way. Absolutely no way. That's the theory it's convenient for women to believe, a certain type of woman, but you got no case. I like women. I idolize women—my whole life is built around women! And women have always liked me too, and that's no bullshit. Let me tell you something, one thing I am definitely *not* is scared of women. (*Pause.*) Confused a little sometimes, maybe. Pissed off a little, okay.

RONDA. And I think scared.

RICKY. Well I think you're the one who's scared, sugartits. What do you say to that?

RONDA. Scared little boy. You live on big schemes and wet dreams.

RICKY. (*Pause.*) What about you, sister? What do *you* live on? (*Silence. She looks away.*)

RONDA. Look, are you gonna eat any of this potato salad, or what?

RICKY. I'm not hungry. (*He opens another beer and sips it, regarding her warily. Crossfade.*)

Scene Two. Saturday Night.

The women's room.

Cheryl, in a slip, is sitting on one of the beds. She is brushing her hair. She stops.

CHERYL. (*Calling offstage.*) Clint! Are you okay?

CLINT. (*Off.*) I'm fine.

CHERYL. (*Pause.*) Are you being sick again?

CLINT. (*Off.*) No, that's stopped, I think. (*She puts down the brush, climbs in bed. She lights a cigarette.*)

CHERYL. Getting a little lonely out here!

CLINT. (*Off.*) In a second! I'm just getting more casual.

CHERYL. Okay. (*After a moment Clint enters, wearing all the same clothes he wore on the beach, including his windbreaker. He is drying his face with a towel.*)

CLINT. Whew, there! Think I got it all. I feel a lot better now.

CHERYL. Good. (*She stubs out her cigarette.*)

CLINT. I washed my face off.

CHERYL. So I see.

CLINT. Their little bar of soap here is really good. I think it's *Palmolive.*

CHERYL. Is it?

CLINT. Yeah, smells great. You want to smell it?

CHERYL. I'll smell it later.

CLINT. It's right in the bathroom. I could get it—only take a second.

CHERYL. Later, okay?

CLINT. Sure, later.

CHERYL. (*Slight pause.*) Are you expecting a storm?

CLINT. Oh yeah. (*Takes off his windbreaker, folds it carefully.*) Guess I won't be needing this.

CHERYL. Feel more casual now?

CLINT. Well, I decided these clothes were actually pretty casual already. These pants are incredibly casual.

CHERYL. Compared to tuxedo pants.

CLINT. Really! So, I thought I'd just wear them a little bit more while we talked, you know. But hey—you certainly don't have to wait for me. You go right ahead and get casual yourself.

CHERYL. I did. I am.

CLINT. You sure are. Ooops, better hang this towel up—it's dripping all over the floor.

CHERYL. Clint.

CLINT. What?

CHERYL. Let it drip.

CLINT. Well it's wood. The floor's wood.

CHERYL. I've paid for the floor.

CLINT. Force of habit, y'know? My mother always used to kill me if I left wet stuff lying around.

CHERYL. Do you see her here?

54

CLINT. (*Pause.*) You think I'm being ridiculous, don't you?

CHERYL. (*Laughing.*) No, I don't, Clint. But there's no reason for you to be so nervous, is there?

CLINT. I'm not nervous!

CHERYL. Don't be afraid of me. I like you—I'm very attracted to you.

CLINT. I'm very attracted to you too.

CHERYL. Okay!

CLINT. Okay. (*She motions for him to sit on the bed. He does so and she begins to rub his shoulders.*)

CHERYL. Maybe these muscles just need a little relaxing . .

CLINT. How *old* do you think this place is? I'm fascinated by the structure.

CHERYL. Clint . . .

CLINT. No, I mean it! I'm not just saying this. I meant to say this when we first came in, because I thought it'd be an interesting topic for conversation.

CHERYL. (*Still massaging.*) Clint—I don't understand this. Half an hour ago you were so forceful! You had me ride up here on your back—remember?

CLINT. Yeah, maybe I hurt it, I don't know. It was further up here than I thought, and it seems like somehow I got less forceful along the way.

CHERYL. How can I convince you it's *okay* to be shy with me. I like your shyness.

CLINT. Sure, your mouth says shy. Your head says jerk.

CHERYL. We don't have to do anything for awhile if that's what's making you feel like this. We could just talk.

CLINT. Aha! The classic thing to say to a jerk! Next you'll say we don't have to do it at all if I don't want to.

CHERYL. No. You *do* have to do it, because *I* want to.

CLINT. So do I! What do you think?

CHERYL. Okay! Don't yell at me. (*She rises, lights another cigarette.*)

CLINT. Maybe I *am* a little nervous. I'll admit that. But try to put yourself in my shoes.

CHERYL. Yours are the only shoes I've been wearing for the last half an hour.

CLINT. You know, you didn't have to pick me.

CHERYL. (*Amazed.*) Well excuse me, buster! I didn't *have* to pick anybody, for your information.

CLINT. I just mean you could've picked Ricky if you wanted somebody who was a big stud or something.

CHERYL. I don't like your friend Ricky very much. He's phoney.

CLINT. I was phoney too, out there.

CHERYL. You weren't as good at it!

CLINT. What do you mean by that?

CHERYL. You were *trying* so hard, and doing so badly, you— I don't know. I liked how silly you were, with all the grokking and everything.

CLINT. Thanks, that cheers me up. You have a lot of these charity activities, or what?

CHERYL. Oh stop it. You made me feel really good about myself, after I was feeling kind of lousy. I don't know how else to explain it. (*Pause.*) Also, I'm attracted to you. Is that so hard to understand?

CLINT. No. (*Pause.*) It's hard to believe, but it isn't hard to understand. (*Pause.*) Shouldn't we be a little worried about leaving Ronda out there with Ricky?

CHERYL. (*Irritably.*) Why?

CLINT. Just seems a little rude for us to go off like this and leave—

CHERYL. It didn't seem so rude to you at the time, goddammit! You want to march back there right now and comfort her, is that it? Fine, go! (*She throws his windbreaker at him.*) Goodbye!

CLINT. Okay, hey, I just—

CHERYL. Ronnie gets on my nerves, okay?! She's determined to have no fun at all and to make me feel guilty as hell whenever I want to have a little of my own, and I'm sick of it! Let her cool off down there for awhile, let her just think about all those wonderful things she called me—it'll do her good! Now enough about her, because I don't want to *hear* it.

CLINT. I'm sorry I brought it up if you're so touchy about it.

CHERYL. (*Loudly.*) I'm not t— (*Pause.*) You know, you're not making this much easier for me. You think I do this all the time, is that what you think?

CLINT. I don't think that.

CHERYL. Yes you do. You think I do this all the time—pick up children or something.

CLINT. I think once in awhile you do maybe. Not all the time. I don't mean children.

CHERYL. You're not a child. You're a full-grown man.

CLINT. Absolutely. I'm in college.

CHERYL. All right.

CLINT. I'm practically a senior.

CHERYL. Then *act* like it. (*She laughs.*) I swear, I never in my whole life had such an impossible time getting a man into bed!

CLINT. You don't know what effect you have on guys. Think about it! I never in my whole life even *touched* somebody that looks like you. (*He sits beside her.*) Cheryl—I stood there in that bathroom trying to figure out how many ways I might screw this thing up, and I couldn't even keep score! It was fun on the beach. I don't want you to think I'm in any way denying the integrity of that experience just because I've turned into warm jello. You made me feel good out there . . . and you make me feel good now. (*Pause.*) I'm sorry if I spoiled your evening.

CHERYL. You know how you make *me* feel right now?

CLINT. How?

CHERYL. Like Mrs. Robinson or something. Like I have to beg you. Well, Clint, it seems to me you're involved in this too. Seems to me you could contribute just a little initiative of your own.

CLINT. (*Pause.*) You don't have to beg me, Cheryl.

CHERYL. I don't?

CLINT. No, you don't. I mean . . . you just don't. (*He leans over, kisses her. He shifts to sit so that he can hug her. His hug is awkward but passionate. She laughs, puts her arms around him. They kiss. Clint softly.*) Jesus.

CHERYL. Yes.

CLINT. Is this really happening to me?

CHERYL. I would say to us.

CLINT. Cause if it isn't, I hope I never wake up.

CHERYL. Clint.

CLINT. What?

CHERYL. Do I have to talk you into taking off your clothes?

CLINT. No! No, I can do that. *That* I can do. (*He scrambles up, begins unbuttoning his shirt. She smiles at him. Crossfade.*)

Scene Three. Saturday Night.

The beach. Ricky and Ronda sitting some distance apart, looking out. She has wrapped the picnic blanket around herself for warmth.

RONDA. See that buoy out there?

RICKY. The silhouette.

RONDA. The moon's so bright it's making shadows from it. See them?

RICKY. Where?

RONDA. See right below it?

RICKY. That's just from the waves.

RONDA. No, that's a shadow. Look.

RICKY. You may be right.

RONDA. (*Pause.*) I love the sound of the waves slapping against that buoy, and the moon coming out of the clouds. So peaceful . . . it reminds me of something, I can't remember what.

RICKY. (*Pause.*) Did you ever see *Jaws*?

RONDA. I wish you hadn't said that.

RICKY. No, it's just—you look at the water, you only see the top, you wonder.

RONDA. I wouldn't go in for a whole summer after that movie.

RICKY. How you ever gonna know what's down there?

RONDA. You can't. Think about how cold it is down there.

RICKY. Think about how dark. (*Pause.*) There's some fish, I forget the name, that lives down like miles, and they've developed their own little flashlight that grows out of their forehead. I read this at the dentist in *National Geographic*. They can never see more than a foot in front of them their whole life, and who even knows how long they live. (*Pause.*) You think this depresses them?

RONDA. I think maybe they don't know the difference.

RICKY. Yeah.

RONDA. Lantern fish.

RICKY. That's the one! How'd you know about them?

RONDA. We must have the same dentist.

RICKY. Yeah, there they are, century after century—just creeping along the bottom with their little flashlights, cruising for algae, checking out the lady fish, and miraculously unchanged from when they were dinosaurs. (*Pause.*) The dumb fucks.

RONDA. It's not the type of lifestyle I would choose if I were a fish.

RICKY. No way.

RONDA. I'd be a marlin.

RICKY. That's a pretty fish.

RONDA. Yeah.

RICKY. I'd be a dolphin.

RONDA. That's not a fish.

RICKY. Sure it is.

RONDA. No, that's a mammal.

RICKY. Get out.

RONDA. Sure. It breathes air.

RICKY. You're crazy. He's got gills, he's a fish.

RONDA. He doesn't have gills.

RICKY. Then how's he breathe, smartass?

RONDA. He's got a hole in his head.

RICKY. Yeah? You too.

RONDA. He breathes air, he's got a hairy body—or at least little bristles—he gives birth to live young, and he nurses them with milk —so he's a mammal! Freshman biology.

RICKY. He gives birth to live young? And nurses them with milk?

RONDA. Yes, he does.

RICKY. Then *he's* not a mammal. He's a hermaphrodite.

RONDA. She does, *she* does.

RICKY. Who!

RONDA. His lady friend.

RICKY. Make up your mind!

RONDA. You drive me crazy!

RICKY. I'm just trying to get you to construct a logical train of thought.

RONDA. You can't stand to lose an argument.

RICKY. I'm still not believing the mama dolphin feeds the kid with milk. For me this is the stumbling block.

RONDA. Well they do.

RICKY. For one thing—where's the tits? You ever see tits on a dolphin?

RONDA. I'm sure they're there. Just because a dolphin doesn't wear a brassiere doesn't mean it hasn't got tits.

RICKY. Uh-huh. And just where does this so-called feeding take place? In a nursery, with a little plastic bottle?

RONDA. In the water, dummy.

RICKY. Right. And what kind of water are we dealing with?

RONDA. Salt water.

RICKY. *Salty*, that's right, and the salty water gets all gooshed up with the milk, yes? —and what kid, even a dolphin, is gonna drink that kind of salty milk? So there's where your theory falls apart.

RONDA. Well since they *live* in it all day long and you don't, maybe they don't *mind* the taste of a little salt water.

RICKY. Sure they don't.

RONDA. Okay!

RICKY. They're crazy about it.

RONDA. There you go.

RICKY. (*Triumphantly.*) Cause they're *fish!*

RONDA. You drive me crazy . . . (*Brief silence.*)

RICKY. You go to college?

RONDA. Yeah. Why?

RICKY. Where'd you go?

RONDA. Little place called Augsburg. You never heard of it.

RICKY. Sure, I heard of it. Two year junior college, co-ed. It's in New Jersey.

RONDA. How'd you know that?

RICKY. You get their business degree?

RONDA. (*Startled.*) Yeah.

RICKY. Where'd you transfer?

RONDA. I didn't. I stopped after two years.

RICKY. (*Surprised.*) You never finished up? (*She shakes her head.*) How come?

RONDA. I don't know.

RICKY. You were *in* college, and you dropped out, but you don't know why?

RONDA. My grades were lousy, how's that?

RICKY. Bullshit.

RONDA. What's that supposed to mean?

RICKY. Bullshit your grades were lousy. From what I've seen, you're a fairly bright chick.

RONDA. You wouldn't think so if you saw my transcript. Besides, after two years I knew I could get a good job at the bank. Why go on?

RICKY. Think I can't tell when I'm being handed a line?

RONDA. Listen, Ricky, I wasn't that crazy about school to begin with, so let's just drop the subject, okay?

RICKY. A college education is a precious thing, not to be taken lightly!

RONDA. Oh, Christ . . .

RICKY. You blew it, Ronda, you know that? (*Pause.*) You're a smart chick, you had a good shot, and you threw it away to work in some lousy bank.

RONDA. I hated college. Now lay off!

RICKY. Where do you come off handing this crap to me? Are we strangers, or what?

RONDA. I had a right to leave whenever I felt like it, for no reason at all!

RICKY. Except you *didn't*, Ronda, and you're still feeding me a line, and I'm not gonna shut up till I find out why!

RONDA. (*Angrily.*) Because my father had a stroke! (*Pause.*) Satisfied? (*Long silence. She fidgets with the picnic basket, and he with a beer can. He pours the remains slowly into the sand, stirs at it with a finger.*)

RICKY. This school you went to—

RONDA. Augsburg!

RICKY. *Augs*burg. (*Pause.*) They have any fraternities?

RONDA. You tell me, since you seem to know so much about college.

RICKY. The catalogues don't always say. (*Gently.*) So I'm asking you.

RONDA. Yes, they did! And every boy I dated there was in one, and they loved it.

RICKY. Which ones they have? They have Deke? Phi Epsilon Pi?

RONDA. All of them.

RICKY. At a junior college?

RONDA. All of them. (*Ricky nods, and then is silent again for awhile. He toys with his empty beer can, looks out to sea.*)

RICKY. Ronda?

RONDA. What?

RICKY. You think if we were to put a message in this beer can and float it out towards Spain, anybody would find it?

RONDA. I don't think anybody looks for messages in beer cans.

RICKY. I guess not.

RONDA. What would our message be?

RICKY. (*Looking out.*) "Fuck . . . you." (*Pause.*) Whatever that is in Spanish. (*He smiles at her. Crossfade.*)

Scene Four. Saturday Night.

The women's room. Clint and Cheryl crowded into one of the narrow beds, under the sheets. They speak softly.

CLINT. Cheryl?

CHERYL. Yes, Clint?

CLINT. (*Pause.*) Did—was it okay, I mean?

CHERYL. You mean did I come?

CLINT. (*Pause.*) Yeah.

CHERYL. Yes, I did.

CLINT. You did?

CHERYL. Yes.

CLINT. (*Pause.*) I made you come?

CHERYL. Sure did. Boom.

CLINT. (*Pause.*) You're not just saying that or anything.

CHERYL. No, Clint.

CLINT. Oh God.

CHERYL. You're sweet. (*She kisses him.*)

CLINT. I can't believe it. That I'm here. That we're here like this! I can't believe how great I feel. I could die this second, and I wouldn't know it. I wouldn't even care.

CHERYL. I would. Cause you know why?

CLINT. Why?

CHERYL. Cause if you got rigor mortis in this position I'd be stuck with you for life.

CLINT. Am I hurting your arm?

CHERYL. No, it's okay.

CLINT. It'll go to sleep.

CHERYL. I'll let you know. (*Silence.*)

CLINT. Cher?

CHERYL. Yes, Clint?

CLINT. I'm really glad you came.

CHERYL. Thank you.

CLINT. (*Pause.*) I came too.

CHERYL. (*Laughing.*) I know. I'm glad.

CLINT. And I just want you to know—you don't have to say anything—I just want you to know this is the most incredible experience I've ever had in my whole life—and I know we can have a fantastic relationship.

CHERYL. (*Slight pause.*) Clint—

CLINT. You don't have to say anything. Cause Cheryl?

CHERYL. Yes?

CLINT. I love you. (*He kisses her, lies back down complacently.*)

CHERYL. (*Slight pause.*) Oh, Clint . . . (*She turns over, looking out in bewilderment. Crossfade.*)

Scene Five. Saturday Night.

The beach. Ronda and Ricky have made a small fire. We see them in its glow.

RICKY. . . . Used to be that getting away from home was the most important thing in the world to me. Getting away from all those numbers your parents pull, and your high school teachers. Boy, getting my own apartment—buying my own groceries, even. Driving your own car for the first time—God, remember that? (*Pause.*) All those things used to seem like such a big deal, but now it seems like it all just gets replaced with other crap. Sometimes I think, getting older—growing up—that's just a matter of getting to think all kinds of things are no longer such a big deal. (*Pause.*) Did you ever feel like you might wake up one day and be too grown up?

RONDA. Me? I'm still amazed I can reach the water fountain.

RICKY. (*Laughs.*) Well, if fucking ever stops being a big deal, I'll blow my brains out. (*She laughs.*) You know when I was little I thought you came the whole time you were having sex? Remember that scene in *A Man and A Woman* where that song's playing and the screen's all red and he's on top of her? I thought he was coming the whole time he was in her. It really scared me when I first started whacking off that it was over so quick.

RONDA. I just couldn't figure out how things fit together. When I swiped my brother's *Playboy* and looked at the women, it was impossible to tell if their hole was any bigger than mine. And I *knew* mine was out of the question.

RICKY. (*Laughs.*) Listen to us! This is incredible. Here we are talking, and it's just like you were a guy!

RONDA. (*Pause.*) I guess I should say thank you.

RICKY. Really, I mean it! No different at all. (*Pause. She is silent, and he realizes he's hurt her feelings.*) Look, I was trying to pay you a compliment.

RONDA. I know that, Ricky.

RICKY. Here you go getting all hard-assed again. I thought maybe

63

we reached a certain level of understanding here tonight. I guess I was wrong.

RONDA. No. You weren't wrong.

RICKY. (*Pause.*) Okay, Ron.

RONDA. Okay.

RICKY. (*Pause.*) I got something I wanted to give you. Here . . . (*He reaches in a pocket of his windbreaker.*)

RONDA. What is it?

RICKY. Key to my motel room. Yours is occupied, so you'll go sleep in mine. (*He offers it.*)

RONDA. (*Takes key; pause.*) What about you?

RICKY. Out here's fine for me.

RONDA. (*Pause.*) Fire's burning low.

RICKY. Yeah.

RONDA. Maybe we should find some more driftwood. (*He looks up at her, she at him steadily. He smiles. Crossfade.*)

Scene Six. Saturday Night.

The women's room. The only light is the dim glow from a bedside lamp. Cheryl lying awake in bed, partly pinned under the sleeping Clint. She tries to shift but cannot because of his weight. She looks down at him, sighs. She strokes his hair, softly.

CHERYL. (*Quietly.*) Hey, Clint. You file your shirts in the closet? (*Pause.*) My boyfriend does. That sounds funny, my boy friend. He's not exactly a boy anymore. Not exactly a friend, either, if you want to know the truth. But he's definitely mine, Clint—in the sense you couldn't pry him away with a crowbar. See, so that's why, when you say you *love* me . . . (*Pause.*) What do you *mean* you love me, anyway? Who *asked* you? Hey, you don't even know me! I was just stringing you along, and you know why? Cause it's fun . . . But who would've thought I'd end up with a guy who was shy and sweet—and short—and in love? (*Pause.*) Listen, uh—I didn't mean that before, about David and the crowbar—that wasn't fair. He's really . . . I mean, he's nice. Oh Jesus, what do you guys *want* from me, anyway? (*Pause.*) Ronnie says I'm Mt. Everest. She says people think because I'm there they have to climb me. (*She laughs.*) Well, give the folks what they want,

64

right? (*Pause.*) But you know . . . it's funny . . . (*Upset.*) I keep telling myself I don't *have* to be Mt. Everest anymore. I mean, I can stop this anytime I feel like it, right? But then it seems like the whole time I keep telling myself that . . . I'm out there piling on the snow, and putting out signs . . . to point the way up. (*Pause. She laughs ruefully to herself.*) So hey! . . . Welcome to the top.

(*Fadeout, with the sound of the surf.*)

Scene Seven. Sunday Morning.

Dawn lights fade up on back cyclorama.

Sound of the surf mixes with cries of gulls.

Lights up slowly on beach, where Ricky and Ronda are asleep. She wears his windbreaker.

Lights up on Clint dressing in bedroom. He kisses the sleeping Cheryl, who stirs. Clint goes outside, very pleased with himself. He stretches, crosses down the boardwalk ramp. He reaches the beach area, where he is surprised to see Ricky and Ronda.

CLINT. Hey, Rick—-what are you doing out here? (*Ricky stirs.*) Hey, wake up, Rick.
RICKY. (*Mumbles.*) Hell am I?
CLINT. Out on the beach. What's going on?
RICKY. Oh, it's you . . . good ol' Clint the Splint.
CLINT. Yeah, listen. I gotta talk to you.
RICKY. You sure as hell do.
CLINT. I gotta ask you something.
RICKY. Keep your voice down—you'll wake up Ronnie.
RONDA. (*Mumbles.*) Stop that screaming.
CLINT. Nobody's screaming.
RONDA. Then something's wrong with my head.
RICKY. Morning, Ron.
RONDA. Morning, Ricky.
CLINT. Hiya Ronda!
RONDA. Good morning, dear. Sleep well?

65

CLINT. Yeah, fine.

RONDA. Good, good.

RICKY. (*To Ronda.*) You sleep okay?

RONDA. Great! Just like in a water bed, only with sand instead of water and no bed.

CLINT. So, I see you guys decided to camp out. I notice you had a fire and everything—fantastic!

RONDA. Wanna see my merit badge?

CLINT. Listen, you guys—I thought maybe we'd all go get some breakfast someplace—the four of us.

RONDA. You did, did you?

CLINT. Yeah, what do you say? Flapjacks, o.j.—I'm starving!

RICKY. Clint—Clint—cool out for a sec, okay? (*In the bedroom, Cheryl rises groggily. She will cross to the mirror, react to her appearance, and then go into the bathroom, taking a handful of clothes.*)

RONDA. My hair's all caked with salt.

RICKY. Mine too.

RONDA. Does it look awful?

RICKY. The pits.

RONDA. (*Laughs.*) I'm going up and take a shower.

RICKY. Sure.

RONDA. (*Rises, takes off his windbreaker.*) Hey. I'm really glad.

RICKY. (*Pause.*) Yeah.

RONDA. You don't have to say anything—in front of the wildlife.

RICKY. Nah.

CLINT. What's that supposed to mean, wildlife?

RONDA. (*To Ricky.*) Well . . . bye. (*She tosses Ricky his windbreaker, turns to go. He hesitates and then calls after her.*)

RICKY. Hey, Ron—wait a minute. (*She stops.*) C'mere. (*She crosses.*) What are we, strangers or what? (*He kisses her forehead.*)

RONDA. Have breakfast with me?

RICKY. Sure I will. Now go on up—and don't take any shit. (*Ronda smiles and leaves. She will cross up to the boardwalk and go down along it to the room. She enters the room, expecting to see Cheryl. When she realizes Cheryl is taking a shower, she lies down on one of the beds and waits for her. After Ronda leaves there is an awkward silence between the two men.*)

CLINT. So!

66

RICKY. So?

CLINT. So, you and ol' Ronda, huh? Hey hey hey! (*Pause.*) What do you say?

RICKY. None of you goddam business!

CLINT. Okay! Jeez . . . Don't be such a sore loser.

RICKY. (*Angrily.*) Who says I lost?

CLINT. Okay.

RICKY. (*Pause.*) What about you, jerkwad. You make out?

CLINT. (*Smugly.*) Oh sure. You know.

RICKY. You better not have screwed up.

CLINT. I didn't!

RICKY. Cause if you *got* her, and then proceeded to screw up, I don't even know what.

CLINT. As a matter of fact, we got along great. That's what I wanted to talk to you about.

RICKY. Yeah?

CLINT. Maybe you could give me some advice.

RICKY. On what?

CLINT. Well, Cheryl and I are starting a relationship.

RICKY. (*Slight pause.*) You are.

CLINT. I know what you're gonna say. There's gonna be a lot of problems. A girl like her, she's gonna want to date other guys.

RICKY. Sure.

CLINT. I understand that, it's natural, and I'd never try to stand in her way.

RICKY. That's a very mature attitude, Clint.

CLINT. Thanks.

RICKY. Think it'll be hard with you still in school? I mean, how you ever gonna see each other?

CLINT. I've been giving that some thought. I'll have weekends, and of course there's Thanksgiving and Christmas—and she can come down to school too. By second term I'll be in a frat house, and I can sneak her in there with no trouble.

RICKY. That's good . . .

CLINT. The thing is—and here's where I could really use your advice—it seems to me a relationship like we're gonna have needs a lot of things to bridge the gaps.

RICKY. Yeah.

CLINT. It needs patience, right?

RICKY. You bet.

CLINT. It needs a mature attitude. Understanding.

RICKY. It needs a car, and the answer is no.

CLINT. Just to borrow!

RICKY. No way, Joe College—get your own.

CLINT. You selfish asshole! You're just jealous of our relationship!

RICKY. Are you out of your mind? What relationship? You think a chick like that is gonna waste her time with a nerd like you?

CLINT. She wasn't exactly wasting her time last night, was she?

RICKY. That was last night. This is today.

CLINT. Yeah? Eat your heart out.

RICKY. How much of all this was her idea?

CLINT. Plenty!

RICKY. Uh-huh. What did she say?

CLINT. She said a lot!

RICKY. Like what?

CLINT. Like between the lines!

RICKY. What is *wrong* with you?

CLINT. She doesn't have to say anything—a guy can tell!

RICKY. Why don't you just admit you dreamed this whole thing up?

CLINT. You weren't there—you don't know what it was like!

RICKY. She won't even remember your name, pencil prick.

CLINT. Yeah? Well I don't even *want* your lousy car! You know what you are, you're pathetic! I don't think you're ever gonna figure out that some people are capable of a mature adult relationship! Fucking class clown, that's all you were! Take away high school and what've you got left? Fucking used-*car* salesman— that's all you'll *ever* be! (*Ricky stares at him, shocked. The men separate in silence, aimlessly and awkwardly. During the following scene they will sit, looking out. Cheryl enters the bedroom, having showered and changed. She is surprised to see Ronda sitting on her bed.*)

RONDA. Good morning, Cher.

CHERYL. How long've you been waiting?

RONDA. Since about seven-thirty last night.

CHERYL. Ron—I'm sorry I kept you out of your room. It was a rotten thing to do.

RONDA. Never mind the room! You knew perfectly well it's not the goddam twenty dollar motel room.

CHERYL. I could say I was drunk, Ronnie, or I was just horny, but that wasn't it—I was pissed as hell at you.

RONDA. For what?

CHERYL. For telling me what to do all the time, which you happen to know is the one thing I can't stand. What kind of friendship is that?

RONDA. What kind of friendship is it where you just dump me the minute I'm in your way? And for a stranger, but he's a guy, so that makes it okay?

CHERYL. (*Pause.*) I said it was rotten, and I apologize. But would you please just try to understand how pinned-in I've been feeling, Ron—about David and the bank and everything else? (*Very upset.*) And here come these two guys, making me feel so incredibly *special*—well what would you do?

RONDA. I don't know. (*Pause.*) But I still got left out!

CHERYL. And I'm sorry! But Ron, maybe if you'd just *talk* to one of them for a change, instead of being so *above* them, you might be amazed to find out they're not as awful as you think. Clint ran around all day acting like some little masher, but he turned out to be very sweet.

RONDA. So did Ricky! (*Cheryl looks at her in amazement.*) Don't look so surprised. He was out on the beach too.

CHERYL. All night?

RONDA. Yeah, at least *he* stayed out there. (*Pause.*) And the answer is no, but we did a lot of talking. We built a fire, and we talked all night. And I'm having breakfast with him, too!

CHERYL. Ron, that's great.

RONDA. Yeah, a lot you cared. I could've been carried off by giant lobsters.

CHERYL. I mean it! I had no idea.

RONDA. You never even wondered where I was—you were too busy grokking Clint.

CHERYL. Oh God—you wouldn't believe the night I had.

RONDA. I believe it. And whatever it was, it should've been worse.

CHERYL. He's in love with me.

RONDA. Get out.

CHERYL. I'm not kidding. I'm quote the most incredible experience of his whole life.

RONDA. Well, I guess for a guy who spends an hour over-salting your cole slaw, true love is the next logical step. (*Pause.*) What are you gonna do?

CHERYL. Well, first I'm gonna get some waffles in him. Then I guess we'll have to have a little talk. I don't know, Ron. I realized last night just how tired I'm getting of helping guys stake claims on me. Even David. Especially David . . . (*Pause.*) I'm not a very easy person to be friends with, huh?

RONDA. No. (*Pause.*) But who is, I guess.

CHERYL. Still think it's worth the effort?

RONDA. Maybe. But this coming winter—when you decide it'd be nice for the two of us to get away to some ski lodge—you know, just for some girl time—?

CHERYL. Yeah?

RONDA. Send me a postcard, okay?

CHERYL. (*Laughing.*) You look horrible. Go wash up! I'll put on some makeup, it'll just take a few minutes.

RONDA. That means an hour and a half.

CHERYL. Hurry *up*, already! I'm starving.

RONDA. I'm going! (*Pause.*) Did I tell you I learned to pee on a public beach?

CHERYL. Ron, honestly!

RONDA. That Ricky—so much to offer a girl.

CHERYL. Get out of here! (*Cheryl throws her towel at Ronda, who laughs and goes into the bathroom. Cheryl gets her makeup case and sits on one of the beds, making up. During the following Ronda comes out of the bathroom, wiping her face. She has also changed her clothes. She and Cheryl leave the room and walk down to the end of the boardwalk, where they stop, listening to the men. On the beach, meanwhile, Clint has risen. He crosses towards Ricky.*)

CLINT. Guess this sort of kills it for the summer, huh?

RICKY. Guess so.

CLINT. But like Thanksgiving. You'll come up to school maybe. And then look out, cause we're gonna raise some hell. (*Pause.*) Take in a ballgame or something. (*Pause.*) What do you say— think you could come up one weekend?

RICKY. Actually I'm gonna be pretty busy this fall. We always do a big clearance on last year's models, then I gotta set up the new showroom.

CLINT. Yeah.

RICKY. You know—just asshole work. Like my old man's been doing for thirty-five years.

CLINT. (*Pause.*) I didn't mean what I said.

RICKY. Is that a fact?

CLINT. A guy gets pissed off over a girl, he'll say anything.

RICKY. Some guys.

CLINT. Come on, Rick, we're pals. We both say stuff all the time but we don't mean it. You know me better than that.

RICKY. I used to. (*Pause.*) I don't mind you taking the chick I spotted first. I don't even mind you make some phoney play for my car But when I find out that you always thought I was just some loser—well buddy I mind that.

CLINT. You know that's not true.

RICKY. I don't know what I know anymore.

CLINT. I may've acted stupid, but I was always your friend. (*Pause.*) I'm sorry, Rick, I don't know how else to say it. I wish you'd tell me it was okay.

RICKY. Well . . . maybe I'll think about it.

RONDA. (*From boardwalk.*) Now who's acting stupid? (*The men turn.*)

CHERYL. Yeah, can't you see he means it?

RICKY. You keep out of this! This is between two guys.

RONDA. Oh, well, excuse me. (*To Cheryl, tough masculine voice.*) Dis is between two guys, see?

CHERYL. (*Same voice.*) Oh yeah?

RHONDA. Yeah!

CHERYL. Hey man, don't mess wid me, man!

RONDA. Ya mudda wears army boots!

CHERYL. Oh yeah?

RONDA. Yeah!

CHERYL. Well how'd you like a knuckle sandwich?

RONDA. Oh yeah? You and whose army? (*They laugh.*)

RICKY. Very funny. Why don't you both take a hike?

RONDA. Hey, listen, Rick—can't you guys fight this out over some food?

CHERYL. Yeah, come on. Hot waffles with strawberries.

RONDA. Whipped cream on top?

CHERYL. Blueberry syrup!

RONDA. (*To Cheryl.*) Hey hey hey!

CHERYL. Whattya say?

RICKY. I don't need all this crap, understand?

RONDA. Forget the *crap*—aren't you hungry?

CLINT. Come on, Rick, sounds good to me. A little breakfast— what do you say?

RICKY. (*Pause.*) I'll eat here.

CHERYL. Eat what?

RICKY. There's plenty of good stuff left here. There's potato salad —there's beer—

RONDA. Yup. Feller can make a durn good breakfast on all that.

CHERYL. C'mon, Ricky—give Clint a break.

RONDA. Loosen up.

CLINT. I said I was sorry.

RICKY. (*Pause.*) A guy has his pride. A guy's pride means more to him than waffles.

CHERYL. Okay, have it your way. Come on, everybody, we'll take my car. (*As she and Clint head for the boardwalk, she puts her arm around his shoulder.*) Clint, there's a little something you and I need to talk about . . .

CLINT. Wha's that?

RICKY. (*Yelling after them.*) Ha! What'd I tell you?

CLINT. (*To Ricky.*) Get bent!

RICKY. Guess you won't be needing that car after all! (*Cheryl and Clint exit, her speaking earnestly to him, and him listening in puzzlement. Ronda hangs back with Ricky.*)

RONDA. You know, I'm kind of hurt you won't eat with me. You said you would.

RICKY. This is a matter of principle.

RONDA. I understand. Well, let me get you started. (*She reaches into the picnic litter, and pulls out a container and a plastic fork.*) Here you go—just a little sand in it, comes right off.

RICKY. Thanks.

RONDA. If you change your mind, it doesn't mean a church wedding. It means a stack of waffles.

RICKY. So long, Ron.

RONDA. So long hardass. (*She goes up the boardwalk and exits, tossing a last line over her shoulder.*) Enjoy your potato salad. (*Ricky looks around, a little amazed they actually did leave him behind. Pause. He looks at the potato salad. He digs out a big forkful, chews it mournfully. He makes a pained face.*)

RICKY. Jee-sus. (*Pause. He makes a decision, jumps up, grabbing his windbreaker. He shouts.*) Hey! Hey you guys! Women— whatever! Wait up! (*He runs along the boardwalk and off as the lights fade. Fadeout. End of play.*)

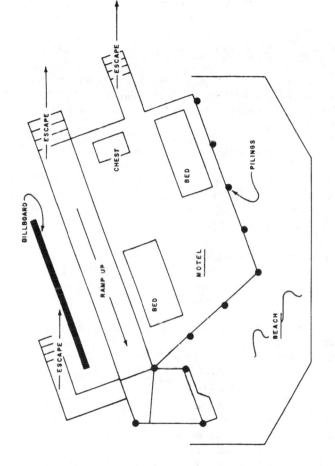

SCENE DESIGN
"HOOTERS"
(DESIGNED BY CHARLES McCARRY)

PROPERTY LIST

ACT ONE

On Stage (in Motel Room)
2 beds with sheets, pillows, bedspreads
Bureau with mirror
2 pole lamps with attached night tables
3 ashtrays (one on each night table, one on bureau)
Pack of matches (by each ashtray)
Box of *Kleenex* (on bureau)

ACT ONE, SCENE 1

Cooler with *Budweiser* and *Coors* beer
2 suitcases—Ricky, *Playboy* magazine in one
1 duffle bag—Clint
Shaving kit in duffle bag
Binoculars in duffle bag

ACT ONE, SCENE 2

Train case with cold cream, assorted makeup, diaphragm case
Tray with hairbrush, nail file on bureau
Suitcase—Cheryl
Straw beach-bag with compact, pretzels, book, suntan lotion, eyeglasses,
    nightgown—Ronda
Handbag with cigarettes, matches, scarf, headband—Cheryl

ACT ONE, SCENE 3

2 beach towels—men
Binoculars
Cooler with *Budweiser* and *Coors*
Radio
Cardboard box with hot dogs
Suntan lotion—Ricky
2 beach towels—women
Beach bag with suntan oil—Cheryl
Straw beach bag—Ronda (from Act One, Scene 2)

Motel towel—Clint
Shaving kit with musk oil, assorted shaving items—Ricky
Clint's clothes in bureau drawer

ACT ONE, SCENE 5

Dress—Cheryl (on bed)
Necklace—Cheryl (on bureau)
Handbag—Cheryl (from Act One, Scene 2)
Tray (on bureau) with bobby pins, gum, cigarettes, matches, *Binaca*,
    lipstick, perfume, comb
Cassette deck
Straw beach bag— Ronda (from Act One, Scene 2)
Train case (from Act One, Scene 2)
Cooler with *Budweiser* and *Coors*
Beach blanket
Picnic basket with *Kentucky Fried Chicken*, vase with flowers, checkered
    tablecloth, 4 paper plates, 4 plastic forks, 4 napkins, container
    cole slaw, container potato salad, container Fried Shrimp, container
    fried clams

ACT TWO

On Stage (in Motel Room)
Hairbrush (on bureau)
Shawl on u. bed
Handbag (Cheryl's) on u. bed
Dress (Cheryl's, from Act One, Scene 5) on u. bed
Cigarette on d. night table
Tray (from Act One, Scene 5) remains on bureau

On Beach
Small fire d. r. (Should plug into concealed outlet in sand)
Checkered tablecloth, covering fire
Beach blanket d. of fire
Picnic basket by blanket
Loose picnic garbage—spread by picnic basket, d. area and r. of motel
    room
Cooler d. l.
Beer cans—d. of cooler

Potato salad in container in picnic basket
1 plastic fork—in picnic basket

ACT TWO, SCENE 2

Motel towel—Clint

ACT TWO, SCENE 5

Uncover fire

Motel room key—Ricky (should be preset in jacket at top of Act Two)

COSTUME PLOT

ACT ONE, SCENE 1

Clint: faded blue jeans, old sneakers, football shirt
Ricky: new blue jeans, red cotton T-shirt, nice shoes

ACT TWO, SCENE 2

Ronda: faded blue jeans, red sleeveless T-shirt, madras pullover blouse, sneakers, white, long flannel nightgown (in straw bag)
Cheryl: white shawl, beige shorts, blue T-shirt with matching short-sleeve jacket, sandals, scarf (knotted at neck)

ACT ONE, SCENE 3

Clint: green gym shorts
Ricky: navy blue tight bikini swimsuit
Ronda: one piece swimsuit, sneakers, beach towel tied around waist, red visor
Cheryl: bikini, blouse (loose, worn over swimsuit), large beach hat, sunglasses, sandals with low heels

ACT ONE, SCENE 4

Clint: bikini underpants, beige jeans, belt, green checkered shirt, sneakers
Ricky: red, white and blue towel tied around torso

ACT ONE, SCENE 5

Ronda: white slacks, blue T-shirt, low-heeled sandals
Cheryl: peach-colored dress, flower on ribbon (tied around neck), stockings, beige high heels
Clint: Same as Act One, Scene 4 with blue windbreaker
Ricky: tan jeans, polyester patterned shirt, beige patent-leather loafers, silver windbreaker

ACT TWO, SCENE 1

Ronda: same as Act One, Scene 5
Ricky: same as Act One, scene 5

77

ACT TWO, SCENE 2

Cheryl: peach slip, stockings
Clint: same as Act One, Scene 5

ACT TWO, SCENE 3

Same as Act Two, Scene 1

ACT TWO, SCENE 4

Cheryl: same as Act Two, Scene 2
Clint: same as Act Two, scene 2, but without shirt and sneakers

ACT TWO, SCENE 5

Same as Act Two, Scene 1

ACT TWO, SCENE 6

Same as Act Two, Scene 2

ACT TWO, SCENE 7

Clint: puts windbreaker back on
Cheryl: (for women's dialogue) same as Act 1, Scene 1
Ronda: (After women's dialogue) peach, long sleeve T-shirt, same pants
  as Act Two, Scene 1
Ricky: same as Act Two, Scene 1, without windbreaker

NEW PLAYS

★ **AT HOME AT THE ZOO by Edward Albee.** Edward Albee delves deeper into his play THE ZOO STORY by adding a first act, HOMELIFE, which precedes Peter's fateful meeting with Jerry on a park bench in Central Park. "An essential and heartening experience." *–NY Times.* "Darkly comic and thrilling." *–Time Out.* "Genuinely fascinating." *–Journal News.* [2M, 1W] ISBN: 978-0-8222-2317-7

★ **PASSING STRANGE book and lyrics by Stew, music by Stew and Heidi Rodewald, created in collaboration with Annie Dorsen.** A daring musical about a young bohemian that takes you from black middle-class America to Amsterdam, Berlin and beyond on a journey towards personal and artistic authenticity. "Fresh, exuberant, bracingly inventive, bitingly funny, and full of heart." *–NY Times.* "The freshest musical in town!" *–Wall Street Journal.* "Excellent songs and a vulnerable heart." *–Variety.* [4M, 3W] ISBN: 978-0-8222-2400-6

★ **REASONS TO BE PRETTY by Neil LaBute.** Greg really, truly adores his girlfriend, Steph. Unfortunately, he also thinks she has a few physical imperfections, and when he mentions them, all hell breaks loose. "Tight, tense and emotionally true." *–Time Magazine.* "Lively and compulsively watchable." *–The Record.* [2M, 2W] ISBN: 978-0-8222-2394-8

★ **OPUS by Michael Hollinger.** With only a few days to rehearse a grueling Beethoven masterpiece, a world-class string quartet struggles to prepare their highest-profile performance ever—a televised ceremony at the White House. "Intimate, intense and profoundly moving." *–Time Out.* "Worthy of scores of bravissimos." *–BroadwayWorld.com.* [4M, 1W] ISBN: 978-0-8222-2363-4

★ **BECKY SHAW by Gina Gionfriddo.** When an evening calculated to bring happiness takes a dark turn, crisis and comedy ensue in this wickedly funny play that asks what we owe the people we love and the strangers who land on our doorstep. "As engrossing as it is ferociously funny." *–NY Times.* "Gionfriddo is some kind of genius." *–Variety.* [2M, 3W] ISBN: 978-0-8222-2402-0

★ **KICKING A DEAD HORSE by Sam Shepard.** Hobart Struther's horse has just dropped dead. In an eighty-minute monologue, he discusses what path brought him here in the first place, the fate of his marriage, his career, politics and eventually the nature of the universe. "Deeply instinctual and intuitive." *–NY Times.* "The brilliance is in the infinite reverberations Shepard extracts from his simple metaphor." *–TheaterMania.* [1M, 1W] ISBN: 978-0-8222-2336-8

DRAMATISTS PLAY SERVICE, INC.
440 Park Avenue South, New York, NY 10016 212-683-8960 Fax 212-213-1539
postmaster@dramatists.com   www.dramatists.com

NEW PLAYS

★ **AUGUST: OSAGE COUNTY by Tracy Letts.** WINNER OF THE 2008 PULITZER PRIZE AND TONY AWARD. When the large Weston family reunites after Dad disappears, their Oklahoma homestead explodes in a maelstrom of repressed truths and unsettling secrets. "Fiercely funny and bitingly sad." –*NY Times.* "Ferociously entertaining." –*Variety.* "A hugely ambitious, highly combustible saga." –*NY Daily News.* [6M, 7W] ISBN: 978-0-8222-2300-9

★ **RUINED by Lynn Nottage.** WINNER OF THE 2009 PULITZER PRIZE. Set in a small mining town in Democratic Republic of Congo, RUINED is a haunting, probing work about the resilience of the human spirit during times of war. "A full-immersion drama of shocking complexity and moral ambiguity." –*Variety.* "Sincere, passionate, courageous." –*Chicago Tribune.* [8M, 4W] ISBN: 978-0-8222-2390-0

★ **GOD OF CARNAGE by Yasmina Reza, translated by Christopher Hampton.** WINNER OF THE 2009 TONY AWARD. A playground altercation between boys brings together their Brooklyn parents, leaving the couples in tatters as the rum flows and tensions explode. "Satisfyingly primitive entertainment." –*NY Times.* "Elegant, acerbic, entertainingly fueled on pure bile." –*Variety.* [2M, 2W] ISBN: 978-0-8222-2399-3

★ **THE SEAFARER by Conor McPherson.** Sharky has returned to Dublin to look after his irascible, aging brother. Old drinking buddies Ivan and Nicky are holed up at the house too, hoping to play some cards. But with the arrival of a stranger from the distant past, the stakes are raised ever higher. "Dark and enthralling Christmas fable." –*NY Times.* "A timeless classic." –*Hollywood Reporter.* [5M] ISBN: 978-0-8222-2284-2

★ **THE NEW CENTURY by Paul Rudnick.** When the playwright is Paul Rudnick, expectations are geared for a play both hilarious and smart, and this provocative and outrageous comedy is no exception. "The one-liners fly like rockets." –*NY Times.* "The funniest playwright around." –*Journal News.* [2M, 3W] ISBN: 978-0-8222-2315-3

★ **SHIPWRECKED! AN ENTERTAINMENT—THE AMAZING ADVENTURES OF LOUIS DE ROUGEMONT (AS TOLD BY HIMSELF) by Donald Margulies.** The amazing story of bravery, survival and celebrity that left nineteenth-century England spellbound. Dare to be whisked away. "A deft, literate narrative." –*LA Times.* "Springs to life like a theatrical pop-up book." –*NY Times.* [2M, 1W] ISBN: 978-0-8222-2341-2

DRAMATISTS PLAY SERVICE, INC.
440 Park Avenue South, New York, NY 10016 212-683-8960 Fax 212-213-1539
postmaster@dramatists.com www.dramatists.com